Ollie

Ollie

Jim Gable

iUniverse, Inc.
Bloomington

Ollie

iUniverse books may be ordered through booksellers or by contacting:

iUniverse
1663 Liberty Drive
Bloomington, IN 47403
www.iuniverse.com
1-800-Authors (1-800-288-4677)

ISBN: 978-1-4620-6704-6 (sc)
ISBN: 978-1-4620-6705-3 (hc)
ISBN: 978-1-4620-6706-0 (ebk)

Printed in the United States of America

iUniverse rev. date: 12/16/2011

Preface

Known by many as a man that feared the Lord, and served Him with great passion, helping others to find their way through a dark world to the kingdom of light, Jim Gable wrote this novel about Ollie. The book, written as fiction, only, because the years gone by created a problem of finding true documentations to established what is truth and to prove it, in all areas of this book.

Ollie, a woman, filled with courage and faith, to overcome a terrible tragedy that happened in her young life. To be blessed to give birth to ten children, five boys and five girls. The individuals in this story, Ollie and Bill, show their love for each other, through their strength, their patience, fortitude, and actual events in their lives. The ordeal with the cow and the birth of her children, along with many names and places are true.

Acknowledgment

I want to thank my wife Shelby, for taking time away from her activities to work with me, helping me to edit my work, to contribute to the writing of this novel with prayers and insight.

Her patience and love has helped me to look ahead, to follow my dream of becoming a writer, so people may enjoy reading my work.

Chapter One

April 1884

The small bent over figure made her way down the old familiar path, now almost overgrown with weeds and vines, to the barn. On her head was a wool cap that was a hand-me-down, made by her grandmother. She pulled it down over her ears to help keep out the cold. The sweater she was wearing had seen many days of hard use. At the elbows, the sweater had holes worn in it. She had rolled the sleeves up above her wrist. Around her waist was a denim cloth apron, which covered the front of her dress. She was never without wearing it. She started her day a couple of hours ago by preparing breakfast for Bill, her husband, and herself. It was not always the easiest thing to do, getting the old wood stove all fired up. However, when the fire did get to going and the stove heated up, Ollie could cook her hoecake white bread. This was the only type of bread she ever cooked for breakfast. Making biscuits took too long with the crowd she had to prepare for down through the years.

It was a cool Tuesday morning, daybreak was about half an hour away, and the night was trying its best to fade away. You could hear nature coming to life all around, and if you stood still and looked long enough, you could almost see it. There was the sound of a rooster crowing somewhere out in the woods, and an owl off in the distance gave an answer back to him. Even with all the children gone from home, she continued to cook the same way for the two of them. Many mornings, you could smell the frying of country sausage and the red eye gravy throughout the old house. She knew how to cook a good breakfast. More times than not, she would cook their dinner as she cooked their breakfast. She never missed an opportunity of trying to accomplish more this day, than she was able to the day before.

Ollie was not always bent-over from broken bones and twisted muscles, which caused her body to be in constant pain. Every step she took was a painful reminder of that fateful morning years ago. Because of that terrible event she has had to hand make all her clothes. It was very difficult to find store bought clothes to fit her twisted body properly. She stood five feet four inches tall at one time, but now, she is less than four feet ten inches.

With her milk pail in one hand, a burning oil lantern in the other, she made her way to the hall of the old barn, which was leaning badly and in need of much repair. Some of the boards around the outside walls were loose on one end and beginning to curl up. Part of the tin roof had turned loose in places and when the wind blew through it, it made a whistling sound you could hear all the way to the house. All the needed repairs were things Bill just hadn't gotten around to doing. The barn, in its own way was crying for help. The screeching of the doors and the rattling of the tin was one way it had of getting your attention. It was slowly creeping off the rock foundation that was stacked up so many years ago on which to build the barn. The livestock didn't mind the barn leaning or the sound of the screeching doors and rattling of the tin roof, it was home to them.

It had been many years since anyone cut hay and stored it in the loft of the barn to have for feeding the livestock. Most of their food now was from the corn and fodder that Bill would take to the mill for grinding into feed. After the harvest of their cotton, he would have the millers at the cotton gin, to grind some of the cottonseeds into a meal. The cow loved to eat this cottonseed meal, more than any other feed, while being milked. Every time Ollie took out some of the meal for feeding, she would take some in her hand and smell the aroma of it. It had such a sweet smell.

For Bill, repairing the barn just seemed easier for him to put it off until another day, since he was now in his senior years. He was not always this slothful. After hanging the lantern on a nail, which Bill had driven into the wall many years ago, she opened the crib door where the feed for the cow was stored. She dipped out enough cottonseed meal to satisfy the cow's appetite while she milked her. She put the feed in the trough, sat down on the old wooden stool, which, also, Bill had made for her, and began washing the cow's sack and teats. Resting her head against the cow's side, she puts her fingers around the cow's teats. Gently she squeezes the teats with her knurled fingers. Arthritis had long ago afflicted her and caused her hands to be in this condition. Each squeeze caused pain to run throughout her body. She squeezed the teats as gently as she could, and Nellie, the cow, gladly released her milk.

As she sat there in the partially lit stall, daybreak was trying desperately to break through the cracks in the walls. With her head resting against the warm body of the cow, her mind started drifting back to the time when she was sixteen living in Dawsonville, Georgia with her Pa, Ma, and her older brother Jules. Jules was two years older than she was, and was always picking at her, and trying to pull some kind of prank on her.

One time Jules found a small frog down at the river, and just for the fun of it, he put it in the lunch basket she carried to school. When the dinner bell rang, everyone started opening their lunch basket or bucket to eat their lunch. When Ollie opened her basket and the frog jumped out into her lap, she screamed, as if the school was on fire. The girls started screaming and running out of the classroom, while the boys, laughing their heads off, tried to catch the frog. All the children, of every age and in each class, shared the same classroom, since it was only a one-room building. That prank got Jules a tearing up by the teacher and a good talking to from Pa when he got home that day.

She started remembering many things, especially the different experiences she had shared with her family. She thought of her days with Bill, what they did and talked about and all the things they had been through together. Memories of her past came flooding into her mind like water pouring over a broken dam. She thought back to the days of her early teens. Of the morning, when she was awaken by her Pa, Edward Voyles, and he told her to rise up and help her brother, Jules, with the feeding of the livestock, and the scattering of the corn in the yard for the chickens.

She remembered how wonderful it was to awake back then, without pain in her body, to be able to stand up straight, walk, and run and play with the children of her age.

———◆———

Ollie was born not too far from this farm. It was on a hundred and fifty acres of prime farmland, which had been in the Voyles family for over a hundred years. Forty acres lay close to Little River making that land the best area for raising corn. The higher ground was better for cotton, tobacco, rye, and the other crops that Ed would decide to plant. There were pecan trees all around the house, and in the yard were all kinds of flowers. Martha, her Ma, had managed to keep some of the flower seeds down through the years. When the flowers were in bloom, they made the home such a beautiful place, that any artist would want to paint it.

"Ollie," said her Pa, "after you and Jules get through feeding the livestock, I want you to help your Ma with the washing of the clothes, instead of going to the field with Jules and me today. Your Ma isn't feeling too well; she could use your help."

"Yes sir, Pa," she replied, thinking how wonderful it will be to spend the day at home with her Ma. This was all new for her, because she usually went to the fields to work with the men. Edward, (most people called him Ed), was a big man, with extra broad shoulders. He could lift one end of a bail of cotton with no problem, none whatsoever. Even he, himself, didn't know how strong he was. He stood six foot three inches tall and the muscles in his arms were so huge, Martha had to make all the sleeves in his shirts extra-large. When he would take off his hat, which was very seldom, you looked at a head covered with wavy reddish brown hair. His hair would curl up around his hat as it sat on his head. He was very handsome. No one dared to mess with him in any way, yet he was a very gentle person.

Jules headed for the barn to pitch down some hay for the horses and cows, while Ollie threw out shelled corn for the chickens, ducks and guineas. Ma brought out a bucket of slop and sat it on the porch for one of them to feed to the hogs. More times than not, that chore fell to Ollie. She did not mind. She always carried on a conversation with them as she gave them their food. She would put some of the shelled corn into her dress pockets, and the hogs would come running to eat it out of her hands. All of her everyday dresses had front pockets on them. Ma's was the same way for you never knew when you would need extra carrying space. Therefore, when Ma made their dresses, she always put a pocket on the left and another one on the right side of the skirt of their dresses.

It didn't take Jules long to feed the livestock and Ollie fed the hogs and chickens. While she was feeding the chickens, she would reach down and picked up one of the bantam hens, as she rubbed her hand down the back of its neck, she would say, "Good morning and how are you today?" then she would sit it back down. She had a way with the animals around the farm, especially the smaller ones. As she got close to the pigpen, the hogs raised a fuss. She would take time to rub them on their heads and down their back, and then they would settle down. Just about every morning when she fed the chickens, the little bantam rooster would throw out his chest and crow several times, just as loud as he could. It was his way of saying, "thank you." He only crowed for Ollie. When anyone else did the feeding, he would eat and be quiet.

Almost every morning, Ollie would go through this thing with Jules. The moment they were through feeding all the animals, he would start chasing her around in the yard, trying to pull her long braided hair, which hung down her back to her waist. She always tried to pay him back by throwing some of the shelled corn at him as she ran toward the house. It was the same every day. If he ever caught her near the water bucket, he would pretend to want a drink of water, but when he got the dipper from her, he only tried to dash her with the water.

The chase ended, when they finally stepped upon the porch of the house, but Jules could not resist trying one more time to pull Ollie's long braids. When he did manage to get his hand on her hair, he would pull her head backwards. Many times, she was able to turn around and face him. When she could, she would fill his thick bushy hair with the cracked corn she still had in her pockets. When he turned her loose to brush the corn out of his hair, she would make a dash for the kitchen. She knew her Pa would be sitting there, and that always ended the pranks. Whenever Jules tried to outdo her, she would find refuge close to her Pa.

"Well I see you two have finished your chores," chuckled Ed.

———◆———

Entering the kitchen, you could smell the aroma of country ham frying and the homemade biscuits taken from the old wood burning stove. Throughout the kitchen was furniture Ed had made down through the years. There was the bread cabinet located next to the stove, and on the next wall was the table he had made for Martha, on which she could keep her mixing bowl. The flour bin he had mounted underneath the table.

He had made the wooden meat box and placed it as far away from the stove as possible. You didn't want the meat to get too warm, even though it was packed away in salt. Her pots and pans hung from the ceiling over the stove. She wanted everything handy and easy to get to, when she started to cook their meals.

When the gravy and eggs were cooked, it was time to eat. As they sat down to eat, Ed said, "Martha, you just outdid yourself this morning. This is the finest meal, I do believe, you have ever prepared."

"Ed, you say that all the time."

"Pa's right Ma," said Jules, filling his plate. "I'll have to work extra hard today for all these biscuits I'm fixing to eat. I can't leave the table till I've filled some of them with your pear preserves."

The pears had come from the tree close to the house, and there were other pear trees out in the pasture. They were always hanging full during harvest time. The livestock enjoyed most of the pears from the trees in the pasture, but there were plenty to go around. After Ma got all she wanted, the livestock could have the rest. In addition, there was an apple tree not too far from the barn. The horses had themselves a time eating the apples, whenever Ed would let them roam in the yard.

"I'll help you find a way to work off some of these biscuits," said Pa.

After breakfast was over, Ed got up from the table; he kissed Martha on her cheek and gently pulled on Ollie's long jet-black hair. Martha was a small person, especially when compared to the size of Ed. She wore her coal black hair done up in a bun held tightly by a comb at the nape of her neck. When she took her hair down to brush and comb it, the length of it was below her knees. Ollie was very much like her mother. They both loved long dresses with flowery designs. Martha was very choosy when she bought cloth for their dresses. She wanted pretty colors with designs of flowers in the material, since she made most of her and Ollie's clothes.

◆

The two men stepped out on the porch and headed for the barn. Jules was six feet tall and weighed two hundred pounds. He had many features like his Pa, with large muscles in his arms and a strong back. He favored his Pa a lot. Together, they could lift just about anything around the farm. Both men wore overalls covered with patches that Martha had used to mend all the holes worn in them. It wasn't anything for them to work ten, maybe, twelve hours on any given day, especially during planting and harvesting time.

"Jules," said Ed, as he put his arm around the young man's shoulder, and looking him in the eyes, "I want you to work Big John today; he needs someone like you to keep up with him." Big John was a large gray and black horse, weighing about fourteen hundred pounds, and acted as if he could out work anyone. The horse was like Ed though, which was very gentle. He would let anyone ride him, but when it came to plowing, he could out do any horse around.

"Yes sir Pa," said Jules. It really didn't matter to him which one he plowed. He just wanted to get it done, so he could spend some time down on Little River fishing and seining. For Jules, there wasn't anything better than having a plate full of fresh cooked catfish. He knew his Ma could cook' um up and fix corn cakes to go with them too.

"I'll plow Belle; she's about my gait today." Belle, the mare, was much smaller of the two horses. She had red hair on her body and white stocking feet. Ed had bought the small horse, because it was the one Martha wanted. He remembered the day they went to town, and to the livestock barn to buy some horses. He knew she had her mind made up before they left home.

"The last time I worked Big John he showed himself. He wore me out in about six hours. The rest of the day, he pulled the plow and me. Oh yeah, Ollie," hollered Pa, looking back toward the house, "don't get to comfortable being at home today. We'll need you in the field tomorrow. We'll be dropping seed." Dropping seed was one important job on the farm. For one thing, you don't ever want to over drop your seeds.

Dropping more than one seed at a time would only create more work for you. You would have to go back and thin out the extra plants, when the seeds came up and began to grow. The other reason, it was a waste of seeds. Pa always saved seeds from one year to the next, but occasionally, he would still have to buy some from the store.

All her growing up years, Ollie had worked alongside of Jules. Even though he was two years older than she was and much stronger, she still could make as many steps as he could, when they worked together. She was thrilled to be staying at home today. This was a first for her to have a day all alone with just her Ma.

After doing the dishes, washing up all the pots and pans, came the job of putting the things away. Ollie could not reach up high enough to hang up the pots and pans. Martha had to put them away. As Ollie began clearing the table, she started humming a tune from one of the songs she had learned at church.

Ed had installed one of those store bought hand pumps he had bought from a manufacturing company in New York. He saw it in a catalog at one of the stores in Dawsonville, and had the storeowner to order it for him. It took him a while to install it. There were quite a few letters exchanged between him and the company, before he actually got the water pumping into the house. The main thing Ed was not doing; he was not priming the pump, before trying to pump the water. It was a great day for everyone, especially Martha, when the water came out of the end of the pump head. The whole family was in the kitchen to see the great event. The moment the water hit the pan, which Ma had placed under the pump head, shouts went up. Ed grabbed Martha, and they danced a little jig around the table. He wanted the well pump in the house, so during the winter months, they wouldn't need to go out on the porch to draw water in the cold weather. In the summer, it was not so bad, but in the winter, it was terrible at times. They had drawn many buckets of water from the well on the porch, so they knew how cold it could get.

Ollie took the broom made out of field straw and swept the kitchen. This chore was something you did every day, because of all the coming and going in and out of the house, much dirt and dust accumulated on the floors. A lot of the dust and dirt fell through the cracks in the floor as you swept. Ed was a good carpenter, among all the other things he could do, but there was no way he could lay the boards of the floor tight enough to close up all the small cracks. He had used a wooden plane to straighten the boards as well as he could.

After they finished cleaning the kitchen, they headed for the bedrooms to strip the beds of the sheets for the regular washday. The weekly wash consisted of a week's worth of all their dirty clothes they had worn and all the bed linens.

"Ollie, it was no coincidence your Pa wanted you to stay with me today. I wanted the time to talk with you when there would be no men folks around. So I asked your Pa to let you stay home with me," Ma said, setting down on the edge of the bed.

"What about?" asked Ollie, as she pulled at the sheets on one of the beds.

"Well, Honey," said Ma, as she stood up and started helping her pull the sheets off the bed. "You're sixteen now and your Pa and I have decided it's time to let you start having some young men callers, if you want to. There are many young men coming to church now, and if any of them ask to call on you, you will have the freedom of saying yes or no. You are no longer a child. You have become a fine young woman. Out here on the farm, things are different from being in town. We hardly see any young folks this far out.

"When I met your Pa it was quite an experience for me. My Pa, your Grandpa Tucker, took me with him to look at some mules the Voyles' had for sell at their farm. When we got there that morning, Mr. Voyles wouldn't hear about no mule talk until we came in and set a spell. Your Pa was out at the back of the house splitting up wood for the stove. Mrs. Voyles had some of her old fashion syrup cookies setting on the table as a treat for all of us; she had made them the day before. We sat around the table talking about what was going on around the farms, and how the weather was treating everybody.

"Mrs. Voyles stepped out on the back porch and called Ed to come into the house to meet us. Your Pa was a good looking young man, and still is," said Martha laughing, wadding up the sheets and tucking them under her arms. "What I want to say to you is there are more young men today for you young women to look at, and you have many more choices, than when I was growing up. Your Pa was an only child, and even though we have had a wonderful marriage and two wonderful children; we really didn't have much of a choice. After we were married, we looked back on that day that my Pa and me went to their farm to buy mules and came home without them. We have always believed the two families planned the whole thing. It was a way of getting your Pa and me together. It wasn't love at first sight, but I do love your Pa, very much."

———❖———

"But I don't need, or want no men callers. I'm happy with just being home with you, Pa, and Jules. You're all that I need or will ever need."

"Ollie, take this mirror and look at yourself real good," said Ma, picking the mirror up off the dresser and handing it to her. "There's not a single young man around that wouldn't want to court you."

She reached out and took the mirror. Very sheepishly, she began to look at herself as her Ma had told her to. Ma was right. She had filled out all those flat places in her dress. She never realized just how much until she looked at herself in the mirror. She did know it was beginning to be hard for her to put on her pullover sweaters.

"I'm happy being here with all of you. I don't need any man," said Ollie, giving the mirror back to her Ma.

"Nonsense, every young woman needs a man. A good man like your Pa," said Martha, looking at her own self in the mirror, and giving her hair a flip with her hand.

"There's no more left like Pa. You got the last one," said Ollie, with a big grin on her face.

"Well, come Sunday, we are all going to church and if any of them young fellows wants to talk with you, you feel free to talk back to them. I already told your Pa, we need to give you some time to at least look at the young men, for you to get to know them, and they get to know you."

"Well, we'll see." She gathered up the sheets and headed outside to the wash pot. "We'll see, we'll see," she mumbled underneath her breath, but she started thinking, 'I could wear the new dress Ma made for me. No, I don't think so, well maybe. I've never worn it before except here on the farm. This could be a good time to show everyone how good Ma is at making dresses. How she is able to use the dress patterns and the cloth she buys from the store in town. Come Sunday, we'll see, we'll see.'

Chapter Two

Jules had cut plenty of wood to go around the iron wash pot, so the fire would heat the water for the wash. The iron wash pot was a hand-me-down from great Grandpa, to Grandpa, now to Pa. There was no telling how many loads of clothes down through the years had been boiled and washed in the old pot. However, they felt sure, there were many more washings left in the old iron pot, and it would last for the next generation or more to come.

Ollie headed to the corner of the house where a big wooden barrel stayed. One day, it took Pa and Jules half of the morning to put the barrel in the right spot to catch the rainwater that came off the roof of the house. They used the water for several things, to wash clothes, water the many flowers Ma had planted in the yard, and for scrubbing the floors in the house. Some of her flowers came from seeds handed down from generation to generation, just like the old wash pot.

It was better than having to pump all the water from the well. It took a lot of water to wash and rinse the clothes. Since Ma was always the one who did the weekly wash, Ollie was very much surprised at how much laundry they had to do. Ma always sorted the clothes into two washings, this she needed to do to get it all done. The light colored clothes were washed first, and then Ma used the same hot water to wash all the dark colored clothes.

"Would you just look at these overalls," said Ma, holding them up for Ollie to see. "Your Pa and Jules are really hard on their clothes." Shaking the dirt and dust out of them, she picked up another pair and said, "These are the ones Jules had on when he tried to corner Blue Boy." (Ma was talking about the hog in the pen.) "I can tell by the looks of their clothes what your Pa and brother did all last week."

As the clothes were boiling in the water, Ollie started singing a song she learned in her Sunday school class a few months back. "Just as I am without one plea," she finished by humming the rest of it. Ma was well pleased to hear her singing and humming the old hymn from church. She knew Ollie had a heart for the Lord. They finally finished with the washing and rinsing of the clothes and headed for the old wire clothesline to hang them up for drying. It took something strong to prop up the clothesline. Ed had cut a limb from an oak tree with a fork in the end of it to be used to push up the clothesline. With all the wet clothes that were hanging on the line, it was all they could do to raise the pole to hang them up.

During the process of hanging up the clothes, Ma said, "Ollie, honey, I want you to know I love you very much. I just want you to take time to look at all the young men and be sure he is the person you want to spend the rest of your life with. We are not trying to marry you off, but we do want you to have a choice."

"I know, Ma, I know." During the rest of the week, she pondered in her heart all the sayings of her Ma.

Sunday morning came with the sun creeping through the windows of Ollie's bedroom. She could hear the birds singing outside, as they were perched in the pecan trees. She got up, put on her clothes and hurried downstairs; then rushed out the door to help Jules feed the livestock. She met Pa as he was coming in from the barn, and he said, "Forget it, honey. Jules and I have already done your chores; you just take your time to make yourself real pretty today."

"Thanks Pa." Whispering underneath her breath she said, "I hope he's not starting to act like Ma." Then she went back into the house. She picked up her dress and pulled it down over her head. She turned around several times looking at herself in the mirror, and was very happy with what she saw. She combed her hair, put on her Sunday go-to-meeting shoes and went down stairs.

After breakfast, Jules and Pa hitched up Big John and Belle to the wagon. Jules installed the seat boards, Pa had made for them to set on, when riding in the wagon. He laid them across the bed of the wagon; then he attached them to the sides of the upright planks on each side. You could install as many of them as needed, it just depended on how many people was going to ride in the wagon.

"All right ladies," yelled Pa, "It's time to leave if you want to get there before everything is over."

"Come and get the food," yelled Martha. "We don't want to go without it. I'm busy helping Ollie get ready."

Ed hopped into the house to get the basket of food on the table, while Jules held the horses. Ma and Ollie finally came out of the house. The two men stared in delight. Never had they seen more beautiful women than the two that stood before them. Jules quickly took the pleasure of helping his Ma and sister up on the seat-boards.

"Ollie, you sure are pretty. Why, you're the prettiest sister I got," said Jules, really meaning it from his heart.

She laughed, knowing she was his only sister and replied, "Why thank you," as she patted his hand for helping her get up on the wagon seat.

"I've never seen such beautiful women as you two are today," said Pa.

Both the women smiled. Blushing, Ollie said, "Thank you, Pa."

Ed took Martha's hand, squeezing it lightly; he moved closer to her on the wagon seat. Ollie did look very beautiful. She was wearing the handmade dress Ma had made for her from the store bought cloth. It fit her well. All her flat places were finally filling out.

The road to the church was narrow and marred with deep ruts due to all the wagons and buggies traveling on it after the recent rains. Just last week the rain was so heavy, that Little River swelled over its banks. There was only one main road going through the country to Dawsonville. All other roads coming from the different farms ran into the main road all along the way. Everyone used it. When the farmers gathered their crops and loaded their wagons to take the harvest to town, all the weight caused the ruts to get deeper and deeper. Often the farmers would follow each other into town, so they could help, if anyone got bogged down in the ruts. In some areas of the road, the farmers would bury their wagons up to their axles.

Ollie was not minding the rough ride this day, for she just turned sixteen, and according to all the things her Ma and Pa told her, she was now a woman and not a child. She was proud to set next to Jules on the wagon seat, even though he still wanted to pull at her hair. He kept a good eye on the basket of food that kept bouncing around every time the wagon wheels went in and out of the deep ruts.

Arriving at the church was exciting. Just about everyone in the rural area attended church, the service was on the first Sunday of each month. Some traveled more than twenty miles away. Everyone brought his or her dinner to spread out for lunch after the service was over. Most used their seat boards from their wagons to make tables to set their food on.

When the people came into the churchyard, they would wave their hands and tip their hats to each other. Ed helped Martha down from the wagon. Making sure her dress was not dragging across the muddy wagon wheels. The other men were busy helping their wives and daughters out of their wagons.

Ollie, standing up in the wagon, straightens her dress out, and takes a quick look out over the churchyard. She saw many of the young men from nearby farms, some in their Sunday go-to-meeting attire, and others in their overalls and Levi jeans. After she had her look, Jules was there to help her out of the wagon. She immediately excused herself from the family, and went over to the well for a drink of water. Most of the young girls and boys hung out at the well, while the smaller children played near the side of the church. At the well, the young women took time to compare themselves to each other. It was an easy way to get away from their parents, using the excuse they needed a drink of water.

Ollie was amazed, as the young men at the well stared at her. It was as if they had never seen her before. However, she knew them all. There were Mr. Paul Crow's two boys, Ron and Lewis, with their sister Inez, Mr. Eddie Long's son, Ben, Mr. Elrod's daughter, Lisa, and son Jacob, and many more she barely knew. Since she just started this past week taking time to look at herself as an adult, she was now taking a second look at the other girls, standing around the well. They too, were filling out all the flat places in their dresses. Some were there for a drink of water; others were there to mingle with the other young folks.

Since she was taking a closer look at the young women, she also took the time to notice some of the young men. Some were wearing light beards with long sideburns; some just had a little fuzz on their faces.

Several of the young men, when they saw Ollie approaching the well, wanted to draw water for her. Two of them started running as fast as they could, trying to be the first one at the well. One was Ron Crow, the other was Jacob Elrod, they both arrived at the well at the same time, each could have won first place. They started squabbling with each other over who got there first, even though they were near Ollie's age. They even got in a pushing and shoving match, as they tried to push the other one away from the well.

While they were busy pushing, shoving, and fussing with each other, another young man, and one in particular, William Franklin, stepped forward and took the rope in his huge hands. He was dressed in patched overalls and a light denim shirt. The brogan shoes he was wearing had seen many days of hard work. He wore a hat cocked on one side of his head exposing some of his wavy light brown hair. His big brown eyes looking through his long eye lashes made a person want to take a second look at the young man. He had managed to be the first to get the rope in his hands. He wanted desperately to draw the water for Ollie.

"May I draw you a drink, Miss Ollie?" asked the young man.

"That would be nice of you," Ollie replied, "and you can drop the Miss, just call me Ollie," as she stepped to the side of the well to be close to where the young man was standing. She took a moment to look him over. Her eyes went up and down from head to toe. She was pleased at what she saw. His patched overalls and the blue denim shirt that was handmade, made him stand out from the rest of the young men. He kept rubbing his well-worn brogan shoes together, trying to keep his legs from shaking. He was so nervous. You could tell from the shoes he was wearing, he was a very strong young man and a hard worker.

"Great," said the young man, taking his hat off, exposing all of his brown, wavy hair. "You can just call me Bill, most folks do."

Ollie was well pleased with the young man with the brown wavy hair. Putting his hat back on his head, he let the bucket down in the well as slow as he could, letting the rope slide through his hands. The church, as of yet, had not put in a windlass for drawing the water. He could tell when the bucket hit the top of the water. While the bucket was filling up, Bill moved as close to her as he could get, and still hold onto the rope. He finally got up enough courage to say, "My, yore dress shore is pretty. Store bought?" he asked.

Ollie wanted to say yes. She wanted to make a great impression on him, but what better way could there be, than to tell him, her Ma had the talent to make the dress she was wearing.

"My Ma made it for me. Ma can make anything she sets her mind to," said Ollie.

"Well it's pretty, and you are pretty too," said Bill, rubbing his brogans on top of each other. He finally pulled the bucket of water out of the well and sat it on a shelf that was there for that purpose. Taking the dipper hanging on the post, he filled it, and offered her a drink. While she was enjoying a cool drink, he asked her a question. "What row are you sitting on in church?" Most of the folks that came to church had a certain place to sit. It was as if that particular seat belonged to them. If you were a stranger coming for the first time (which was hardly ever) you waited until everyone else sat down, then you chose a seat.

"Ma always has our family to sit on the right side of the church, second row from the front," she replied.

"What a coincidence, that's the row I'll be sitting on today." That really was not the truth. Bill always waited until everyone took his or her seat before he sat down, then he would sit down wherever there was an empty seat. However, not this Sunday, he was going to be on the second row from the front on the right hand side.

The organist began to play an old spiritual hymn on the organ, as she pumped air into the bellows with both feet. No one knew just how old the organ was. It just was always there, and no one knew who was responsible for it being there. The church was established and the building built around the eighteenth century. The sweet sound coming from the organ was a call to come into God's house to worship.

The people began to seat themselves. Many of the women were wearing their Sunday best, and some had even sewn handmade ribbons on top of their bonnets and around the brim to fancy them up. Just about all the men were wearing their overalls. The Voyles family came into the church, and just as Ollie had told Bill, they chose to sit on the right side, second row from the front. Bill had told Ollie; he had chosen to sit there too. There was always an order in which the Voyles family followed as they sit down in the pew. Jules went in first, then Ollie, next Martha, and last Ed. He always wanted to set on the outside next to the center aisle. However, this Sunday Ollie made a change to the Voyles tradition. Instead of her sitting next to Ma, she insisted that Jules swap places with her, so

16

she could be next to Bill. Jules, trying to play with Ollie, and teasing her about the new arrangement, just for a moment, he refused to swap places with her. Pa seeing what was going on, cleared his throat a few times, and without a word spoken, Jules swapped places with her, moving over next to his Ma, with a smirk on his face.

Mrs. Katie McClure, the organist, could really play the organ. You couldn't mention a hymn that she didn't know how to play. Many times, in jester, someone would say that, they thought she came with the organ. However, after everything was said and done she was the only one in the community who knew how to play all the hymns. When she began pumping the old organ with her feet, she had to pull her dress up enough so it would not hang on the pedals. This exposed her high top socks above the ankle boots. Her arms seemed to float up and down with the puffed sleeve blouse she had on, each time she struck the keyboard. Her high-pitched voice rang out the spiritual hymn, "What a Friend We Have in Jesus." Ollie and Bill missed half the words just glancing at each other. He was sitting about a foot away from her when the service first started. By the time, Pastor Mosley was half way through his sermon Bill had wiggled his way to within inches of her. As he tapped his brogans to the music, he made it a point to touch her shoes with every other beat. Ollie didn't mind. This was the first time a young man had paid her so much attention, and she was enjoying every moment of it. They never spoke to each other during the singing or the preaching. The service was finally over, and everybody stood up and headed for the door. Many were shaking hands with the minister as they passed by telling him how great his sermon was.

"Reverend," said Paul Crow as he passed by and shook hands, "You sure know how to keep people on their toes. I never once took my eyes off you this morning."

"That's fine," said the pastor, smiling. "I was, also, able to help some catch a nap or two."

Through the crowd, Ollie lost sight of Bill. She was so short she couldn't see over the heads of the others. She quickly made up her mind, he had already left the church and headed for home. Disappointed, she slowly made her way out into the churchyard. To her happy surprise, he was standing at the front of their wagon rubbing the head of Big John. She was so pleased to see that he did not leave.

"I didn't want to wait till everyone left the church," said Bill, tucking his shirt tighter in his overalls. "I wanted to make sure I was here first at your wagon. The way the other fellows were eyeing you, I was afraid they would beat me here."

"Well, they didn't," said Ollie, her mouth so dry that her voice squeaked. She too, like Bill, was nervous; she kept pulling at the sleeves of her dress. Flipping back her long black hair, she finally got out the words, "Would you like to have dinner with us? Ma always fixes plenty of food. She has a saying, 'you never know who will share a meal with you, so always have enough for them'."

"That sure is nice of you to ask, I would be pleased too."

She was very pleased he said yes. For the first time in her life, she was talking as an adult. It was so different. Before, on the Sunday church days, she would talk with the other girls about what they had been doing and the games they had played during the past month. Today she was talking to a young man, which made her nervous and caused her heart to beat fast. Now she would have time to find out more about him. She was already pleased and happy with how he addressed her, with his manners, and the attention he was showing her. The other young girls and boys were pairing off, talking and poking fun at each other, as she had done in the past.

Ed and Martha took the basket of food from the wagon and headed for the wooden tables under the big oak trees. Martha had prepared a medium basket full of fried chicken with a large bowl of gravy wrapped in a heavy cloth trying to keep it warm. She also fixed boil corn on the cob, green beans with small Irish potatoes cooked with them. She had prepared two gallons of tea and baked a sweet potato custard. Jules always made sure he put some of Ma's pickles in the basket. Ed always brought a gallon of his homemade muscadine wine to share with the others.

Most everyone brought food and stayed to have dinner together. Here was the time and place everybody caught up on the latest news with their neighbors, and either told or just listened to the latest gossip. Either way, no one left until it was all over, this was usually late in the evening. After everyone finished eating and put their food away, they went from family to family, either sharing the news they knew or listening to what the other folks had to say. The men were always talking about how their farms and crops were doing. The women mostly talked about what their men folks was doing or not doing.

Eddie Long began telling how he was in Dawsonville awhile back and how he had swapped one of his prime calves to a fella named Elmer Jones for a fiddle. In the swap, Elmer agreed to teach him how to play it.

The young folks gathered in different groups, and the smaller ones ran and played tag and hide and seek. One of the children tied a can to a hound dog's tail. The dog had followed the family to church, and he was running in every direction trying to get the can loose from his tail. The children were laughing and having fun chasing him.

Eddie was good as his word. He went to his wagon and took down an old worn fiddle case. Opening it up, he took out the fiddle he had traded for. After tuning some of the strings, he encouraged everyone to gather around for a square dance. This was great news for the children. The adults knew the children always came first, and wanted them to have some fun. Harris Elrod, Jacob's father, always brought his banjo to play. He was glad to have someone to play with him, even if he was an amateur. Together they started playing some good dancing music. The people began clapping their hands and stomping their feet as the music rang out among them. Most everyone could enjoy a good old fashion square dance. Then an older man stepped out of the crowd and started calling the dance.

"Grab your partner and let's get started," he said.

The children didn't hesitate. They formed a circle and around they went, making moves to the music, as the old timer called the dance. It didn't matter to them whether they were dancing with someone or just dancing by themselves. They were enjoying their time on the dance floor. They yelled and screamed with laughter, never minding that some of them were dragging their partners, instead of dancing with them.

Soon it was the adults turn. Ed took Martha by the hand; they started dancing to the call of the old timer. The other farmers joined in and danced with their wives or daughters. After swinging your partner, and going back and forth, swapping them in and out with someone else, and doing the do-si-do, you were ready to stop and rest awhile. By the time everyone had danced a dance or two, they were ready to sit for a spell and let the dust settle. Several of the men and women took Ed's invite to try out his new wine down at the end of the table. Even the pastor had to try it.

Chapter Three

All afternoon Ollie and Bill strolled around the church grounds. Never out of sight of the people, but yet all alone with each other. Neither one could keep their eyes off the other. If this was what people called courting, then she was enjoying every minute of it. Bill would stoop down every so often and pick up a stone and toss it out a cross the yard. Ollie would kick the bottom of her dress causing it to flare out as she walked along. The other young adult girls and boys had paired up, some in groups; others were walking and talking, just like Ollie and Bill. Inez Crow and Lisa Elrod were at the well talking to a young man named Ben. The young girls liked Ben, because he pretty well knew all the dance steps. His Pa would play for him at home, where he could learn all the new dances.

Ollie and Bill managed to drift a little further away from the crowd, but always making sure they were in sight of the elders. There were many varieties of wild flowers blooming around the church. Several of the farmer's wives had brought some of their flowers from home and planted them in the churchyard, where everyone could enjoy them.

Several times Bill would stop to pick one of the flowers for Ollie. In the past, she had always picked some of the flowers and gave them to her Ma. Now, a young man was giving flowers to her along with all his attention. She really didn't know what to say or do. She only knew she was extremely happy by all the attention she was getting. They strolled down to the creek that flowed near the church. The water was eddy in this area as it passed by the church flowing toward a bend in the creek. The bend created a large pool of deep water where the grown-ups went swimming many times after dinner on church Sundays. The smaller children played in the shallow water up the creek, so they sat down on the bank to watch the children as they played in the water.

"Would you like to go swimming?" he asked.

"No. I don't know how to swim," Ollie replied.

"You don't know how to swim? I thought everybody knew how to swim," said Bill, laughing.

"When did you learn how to swim?" she asked.

"I'm not sure just when, but I remember the first experience I had. I was with Grandpa Franklin. We were coming back from town in his wagon. It had rained a lot that week and Grandpa stopped the mule and wagon in the middle of the bridge to watch the water flow down Little River. It had risen about two feet above normal and was still rising. Curious as I was, I got out of the wagon to take a closer look. There were limbs and leaves in the water. I was holding on to the banister rail looking down into the water, when my hand slipped. Grandpa had told me several times to be careful and not to get to close to the edge of the bridge. I thought I was doing okay until I fell into the water. I started screaming for help. The force of the water carried me downstream; Grandpa was not able to help me. He had gotten too old to be jumping into a flooded river. By the time, he got down out of the wagon I was several hundred yards downstream. The weight of my overalls and shoes quickly took me under. When I came up, in sure panic, I began slapping my arms, and kicking my legs, with all the strength that I had. Then I realized I was keeping myself from going back under the water by doing so. I forced my way over to the edge of the bank and was finally able to climb out of the river. I was a long way down the river. That's how I learned how to swim."

"Don't go no further," were the next words Ollie and Bill heard. Some of the children were yelling at the eight-year-old child, named Joann. She had wandered too far away from the other children in the eddy water and the swift current was taking her downstream. It was pulling her toward the swimming hole in the bend of the creek. The younger children started making their way out of the water. They were scared as they saw their young friend going toward the deeper water. The children on the bank were screaming as loud as they could for the young girl to turn around and come back up stream.

"Turn around! Come back!" the children were yelling. Some of them started running back toward the church where the adults were, to tell them about Joann.

Bill and Ollie quickly stood up and they joined in with the children, shouting for Joann to stop, turn around, and come back up stream.

"Don't go any further," yelled Bill, as loud as he could, running down the bank toward the swimming hole.

It was too late. Joann was hearing the shouts of all the children and Bill, but had reached a place in the creek where the current was stronger than she was. The screaming children running toward the church got the attention of the grownups, but it was too late. They were too far away for any of them to help Joann now. The swift current had pulled her into the deepest part of the swimming hole. When she went under the water for the first time, Bill, frantically snatched off his brogans and without hesitation he dove into the water, clothes and all. He started swimming as fast as he could to get to the area where he saw her go under. His heavy wet clothes were holding him down in such a way; that it was causing him to fight to stay above the water. He managed to get to the middle of the swimming hole, and from there he could look all around to see if Joann would surface again. He was struggling with all his strength to stay on top of the water, so he could see what was going on. Joann finally came to the surface the second time.

When Bill saw her, he made a grab for her. She was going down again. He finally managed to grab her hands. As she went down for the third time, he grabbed her by the hair of her head and they both went under. He would not let go of her. With his heavy wet clothes on, he was having a hard time trying to swim to shallow water, but in his desperation, he would not let her go. They both went deeper into the water. Finally, he felt his feet touch the bottom of the creek. When he did, still holding onto Joann's hair, he started walking under water. He came walking out of the deep swimming hole into shallow water, dragging her behind him.

By this time, all the folks from church were down at the bank of the creek. Some were praying, "Oh God help them, Lord spare them," others were hollering, "Where are you, where are you?"

Some of the men jumped into the creek, when they saw Bill with Joann. Getting to them as quickly as they could, they helped to pull them out of the water and up the bank. With tears flowing down her cheeks,

Ollie said, "Oh Bill, I was never so scared in all my life," as she grabbed hold of his hand.

Joann's Mom and Dad ran quickly to the creek. They got there in time to see her being lifted out of the water and placed upon the bank by the men. Rushing over to her, Virgil picked her up and held her in his arms. Stroking her hair with his hand and crying, he said to Bill, "That was a very courageous thing you did young man. We will be forever in your debt."

"Thank the good Lord you're safe," said Lily, taking Joann from Virgil's arms. She sat down on the ground, and with her hands wiped the water from her face, as she tried to dry her hair with the tail of her skirt.

Everyone came around to shake Bill's hands and pat him on the back, as they showered him with words of praise and called him a hero. Ollie was so proud of him. She would not let go of his hand as they walked back to the churchyard. That was the greatest reward for him, having her by his side and holding his hand.

"Bill, I've got some extra clothes in the back room of the church," said Pastor Mosley. "You can change into them if you like. I keep some extra clothes here, just in case someone has a heart change, and wants to get baptized."

"Thank you sir," Bill replied, "I'll take you up on it." After he changed his clothes, he came back outside. Someone had found his shoes and brought them to him. After putting them on, he went to find Ollie.

Everyone was rejoicing and having a good time. None of the children wanted to go back and play in the water, at least not today. He found Ollie waiting for him at the well. She was trying desperately not to show her true feelings, but wasn't doing a very good job of hiding them.

"How are you doing? Are you alright?" she asked.

"I feel much better now. Getting into dry clothes always makes a person feel better. You want to walk back toward the creek?" he asked, seeing that everyone had left the creek and was near the church. He felt like they could be alone there.

"That would be really nice," Ollie replied.

As they slowly walked along, Bill picked up a few stones that were in their path. When they were close to the water, he reared back and scaled one of them across the water. It took a high bounce, as it first touched the water, and then went tippy toeing plumb across to the other side. Ollie was amazed at how the stone danced across the water. He was pleased to see that simple things brought delight to her face.

"Would you like to try it?" asked Bill, hoping she would say yes.

"I've never seen anyone do that before," she replied. "I don't know how you did it."

"Here, let me show you," he said, moving much closer to her. He put the stone in her right hand, and told her to hold it between her forefinger and her thumb. He held her hand as long as he could, and then finally said, "Try to make the stone land on top of the water as flat as you can, when you throw it. OK?"

"OK," she replied, as she wound up and threw the stone toward the water. The stone went straight into the water without one bounce, but it gave them a good laugh.

"That one had no intention of flying across the water," she said.

"Here, try another one. Try again to make it land as flat on the water as you can."

"OK, I'll try," she replied, as she wound up her arm and released the stone toward the creek. To her surprise, when the stone hit the water it took a big bounce, along with a few short ones, before disappearing underneath the water. She jumped up and down, yelling, "I did it, I did it." He loved the joyful childlike reaction he saw in her.

Walking back toward the church, Bill picked up a small stick and carried it with him tapping it to the side of his leg ever so often. Ollie picked a few more of the flowers that were blooming near the side of the church. As they walked around, she lifted the flowers to her nose for a moment to smell them, and then she asked him, "would you like to smell the sweetness and the aroma of this one?"

He quickly answered yes. He was willing to do anything that would bring him close to her. They were unsure how to have a conversation with each other, as both were very backward and courting was something new. Up until now, she was always around the other young girls, and he being an only child, was always where his Pa was. Bill had always taken part in the square dancing, when Mr. Elrod brought his banjo and played.

However, this time he didn't seem interested in dancing, as he and Ollie was so busy getting acquainted with each other, but he could tell by the way she was swaying her body she liked the music.

It was now late in the evening and the women were beginning to put their things together to head home. For some, the distance was quite long. The Voyles family put their baskets of leftover food in the wagon, and Ed climbed aboard to hold the horses, leaving Jules to help the women up into the wagon. Bill stepped forward, reached out his hand to help Ollie up on the wagon seat. When she placed her hand in his, it felt lost, for his hands were very large. He was tall, thin, and very strong for a young man, and towered above her by a foot. Ollie, even stretching out as much as she could, was not much over five feet four inches tall. Bill's hands were rough and callused, because of all the hard work he did on the farm. Yet, she could feel the tenderness in his hands as he helped her into the wagon.

"Well Ollie," said Ma as she came near the wagon with Jules right beside her, "I see you have found a gentleman who knows how to help a lady."

"Ma, Bill's folks tend the farm across Little River," she said.

"Yes I know. Your Pa and I met the Franklin's one day in Dawsonville. I think we both were looking at the same milk cow that was for sell."

"That was year before last," said Bill. "I remember Pa saying to Ma when he came home 'the Voyles almost bought this little heifer.' She shore is a mighty fine cow. It was nice having dinner with all of you today. I'd like to call on your daughter sometime if it's all right with you folks."

"Well William," began Ma . . .

"Ma," interrupted Ollie, "William likes to be called Bill."

"Well Bill," said Ma, trying to straighten up her hair a bit, which had fallen out of place during the square dance, "It's alright with us, if it's alright with Ollie."

Ollie smiled and softly spoke to Bill and said, "I'll be looking forward to seeing you next church day."

Bill stood motionless, as Jules helped his Ma upon the wagon. Jules turned and shook hands with Bill and climbed aboard. With a few giddy-up words from Pa, the horses put their muscles into action and the wagon started rolling out of the churchyard headed for home. As they were slowly going out of sight, Ed turned around in his seat and yelled back to Bill, "Son that was a wonderful thing you did today. The Floyd's will forever be grateful to you and so will everyone else."

As Bill turned to walk away, Pastor Mosley approached him and said, "Son, looks like you sorter like the Voyles' daughter a lot."

"Sure enough Pastor. I'm gonna marry that girl. Yes sir, I'm gonna marry her."

✦

The Franklin farm lays across Little River in the opposite direction from the Voyles farm. It is about a three-maybe four-hour walk, from one farm to the other. The Voyles farm was closer to the church, than the Franklin's farm. Bill headed toward home, walking at a faster pace, than when he came.

Some of the families, such as the Green's and the Weldon's, offered him a ride since they were going in his direction, but he turned them all down. He wanted to walk and be by himself with all his new thoughts about Ollie. He was afraid if he talked about it, the wonderful feeling he had might disappear. He ran, walked, skipped along, sung, whistled, and even tried doing some cartwheels. When he got to Little River, he sat down on the bridge to rest his body, but his mind was racing with the thoughts of her.

"I love that girl," talking aloud to himself, for he knew no one else was around to hear him. He hollered as loud as he could, "I think she likes me too. She might even love me, maybe." Sitting there, his thoughts went back to the creek, and the wonderful time he and Ollie had, as they strolled down and sat on the bank. He could still see her face and hear her laughter in his mind. When he stood up, he felt something in his pocket, to his surprise it was one of the flat stones he had picked up and they had not thrown into the creek. He reared back and threw the stone as far down the river as he could. Each bounce the stone made he could hear Ollie shouting, "I did it, I did it." Then he tucked away his thoughts and proceeded toward home.

It was almost dark when the farmhouse came in sight, which filled his soul with peace. He started walking faster and faster until without realizing it, he was running. As he entered the yard, old Sam, their best hunting dog with two other hounds, began barking and came running out from under the floor of the house. Bill held out his hands and started rubbing and speaking to them, hoping his voice would calm them down. They circled him a few times, as they licked his hands; they were making

26

sure he was someone who should be there. Then they went quietly back under the house to stand guard.

Bill wiped the saliva from the dogs, off his hands, on his pants, and then jumped upon the porch. He could hardly wait to get inside to tell his folks about Ollie. Tom, his Pa, sitting in a straight chair, was enjoying a smoke from his cob pipe, as he worked on a new harness for the mules. Mattie, his Ma, was sitting in an old homemade rocker passed down to her from her Grandmother doing some mending and patchwork on Pa's and his overalls.

"Ma, Pa," said Bill, charging into the house. "You should have gone to church today and seen little Ollie Voyles. She is the prettiest thing I have ever seen. Why, even the dress she had on looked store bought. She said Mrs. Voyles hand made it for her. Can you believe someone could hand make something so fine you thought it was store bought?"

"Well son," replied his Pa, patting his corncob pipe in the palm of his hand, "you know we would have been there if it weren't for the little heifer being so close to dropping her calf. It happened about eleven thirty this morning. It sure is a pretty little thing. You made a great choice, from among the young women, when you chose Ollie to talk with. She and all her family are hard workers. There's not a lazy one among them."

"I agree," said his Ma. "Now set down and have your supper, your Pa and I have already eaten. Whose clothes do you have on anyway? They're certainly not yours."

"I'll tell you all about it after I eat," said Bill. He washed his hands and set down at the table.

Ma got up from her rocker and passed the food to him as she continued talking. "The Voyles are very fine folks. I have always regretted that your Pa bought the cow we now have, because they were looking at it too. Martha wanted it so bad. But your Pa insisted we had to have that cow."

"Now Matt, you know why I bought that cow." He was puffing more smoke from his cob pipe than a train does trying to get started down the track. "We needed one that gave plenty of milk and that's the one we got." Tom often called Mattie, Matt, especially when they wasn't agreeing about things.

"Oh, I know it, but Martha wanted it so bad. She always was a lover of small animals. We could've bought another one, but we didn't." Then she gave Tom one of her low eyebrow looks.

"There are no hard feelings between yaw and them, are they?" asked Bill, pushing his plate aside.

"Land sakes no," said Mattie. "We are the best of friends. I just wished your Pa had let her have the little heifer, that's all. Now tell me, why you are wearing someone else's clothes."

"You know Mr. and Mrs. Floyd's little girl, Joann," said Bill.

"Yes, we know Joann. What about Joann?" asked Tom?

"She almost drowned in the river today in the old swimming hole at the church," said Bill, as he pulled at his shirt, trying to make it stay in the pants he had on.

"What in the world is an eight year old child doing in that swimming hole? Why, that thing must be ten feet deep," said Mattie.

"She wasn't in the swimming hole to start with. She was playing with some of the other children in the shallow water, upstream, away from the swimming hole. She just lost sight of where she was and wandered further downstream than she thought. By the time she realized where she had drifted to, it was too late. The force of the water pulled her further downstream into the deeper water."

"It's a wonder that little child hadn't drown," said Tom, getting up from his chair and coming over to the table and setting down with Bill and Mattie.

"She would have, if someone hadn't been right there at the time. That someone was me. I was at the right place, at the right time, to help save a life. I jumped in after her and managed to pull her out of the swimming hole. With the help of some of the other men, we made it out of the creek. That is why I have on these different clothes. They belong to Pastor Mosley. I changed out of my wet clothes and put on his dry ones."

"Praise the Lord you both are safe," said Mattie, as she came over, put her arms around him and gave him a big hug.

"Well, it's getting late; it's time we turned in. We got lots of work to do tomorrow," said Pa, placing his pipe on the mantel. He never said a word about what his son just told them that happened at the creek.

"If you don't mind, I think I will stay up a little longer," said Bill. "I want to read awhile."

"You stay up as long as you want to son," said Ma, putting his dirty dishes in the basin to wash tomorrow morning. She turned out the lamp in the kitchen. "Just remember to turn out the other lamp when you're through reading."

"Yes ma'am." He walked over and picked up the heavy and worn Bible from the table in the corner of the room. Then he moved close to the lamp, which was near the fireplace. He found in the book of Genesis, the second chapter, where God took a rib from man and made a woman for the man, and then said, "Therefore shall a man leave his father and his mother, and shall cleave unto his wife." He closed the Bible and turned out the lamp. He sat there in the darkness for the longest, pondering all this in his heart, before going to bed.

Chapter Four

Bill was at the barn the next morning at daybreak. He wanted to see the newborn calf. Just as his Pa had said, she was a beautiful little heifer. While he was rubbing the neck of the calf, he could hear the sound of the hound's barking off in the distant as they made their morning rounds. They were hunting dogs. When he or Pa didn't have the time to take them hunting, they would take themselves.

"Breakfast ready," hollered Tom, from the back porch. "Ma wants us sitting down in five minutes."

"Okay," yelled Bill, as he came from the barn. He took the time to wash his hands at the well. Then into the kitchen he went, throwing one leg over his chair as he sat down.

"Those dogs shore does like to hunt," he said, brushing his hair back from his face.

"One of us can check on them after breakfast. They will not leave the area if they have something treed. And they jest might have something treed that we can't do without," laughed Pa.

"Get the blessing said," said Ma, wiping her hands with her apron. "One of you can tend to them dogs later."

Without pausing for one second, Bill started praying. "Dear Lord, we thank you for what we are about to receive, and Lord, make Ollie's heart toward me, like mine is toward her. Amen."

"You really do like that Voyles girl, don't you?" Pa asked.

"Yes sir. I'm gonna marry her. Yep, one day I'm gonna marry her," he repeated.

"Don't you think she might have something to say about that?" asked Ma.

"Yes Ma'am. She will have a lot to say about it, but I'm going to marry her. Yes sir-re. Just wait and see."

"Well, finish your breakfast," said Pa, loading up his pipe with tobacco. "When you are through, you take care of the heifer, while I go and see what's bothering them dogs."

"Yes sir," Bill replied.

Tom took his twelve gauge double barrel shot gun down from over the front door, and took a box of shells from the cabinet next to the door. He took out of the box four or five shells and put them in his over coat pocket.

"I thought you were just going hunting. With all that ammunition you could start a war," said Mattie.

"Well, you just don't know what them dogs may have got themselves into. They have been hollering for quite a long time." Then he put on his hat and headed out the door.

"You be careful. If you're not back soon, I will send Bill out to find you and those dogs," Mattie said.

He stepped off the porch and headed out across the open fields into the woods. He could hear his dogs barking as he followed the sound coming from the river area. Then he climbed over fallen trees and brushes, and jumped a few small streams, just trying to follow the sounds of the dogs. When he got close, he could see two of his hounds circling a large oak tree. A third one was laying on the ground very still. Tom looked the dog over and was shocked to see just how bad he was hurt. His body had deep gashes in it, his head covered with blood; he was bleeding from his ears and side. He had been in a horrific battle with something, and that something had almost killed him. He was still alive, but barely.

The dogs refused to quieten down even though Tom scolded them. They kept looking up into the tree, circling it, and at times, they jumped up and clawed at the trunk of the tree. He had never seen his dogs this mad before. He joined in with the dogs and started looking up into the tree. For a long time, he could see nothing, then, there was one, no there were two, huge raccoons stretched out on a limb high up in the tree. As he would go to one side of the tree, the raccoons would move to the other side. This could go on forever he thought. He knew he would haft to get his wounded dog some help very soon or it would die.

The dogs continuous barking caused the raccoons to move further out on the limb. They were out so far on the limb now that Tom could barely see them. He knew if he didn't try to get them down, his dogs would never give up the hunt. He made up his mind, and then he raised his gun, took the best aim he could, and fired both barrels. To his surprise, both raccoons fell out of the tree. Hitting the ground, one never moved, it was dead. The other was wounded, but still able to put up a good fight with the two remaining dogs. It didn't take those two hounds long to end the long awaited battle.

Tom picked up the wounded dog and tried to carry it, along with his gun. This wasn't working. He stood his gun next to the tree, picked up his dog, and headed for home. Blood from the wounded dog was getting all over his overalls. When he reached the open field, Bill, riding one of the mules, met him.

"We heard the sound of your gun and Ma sent me to check on you."

"I'm glad you did. I need your help. You take the dog back with you," he said, as he lifted the dog up to Bill. "He's been in a fight with two raccoons. I will go back and get my gun."

"Did you get the raccoons?" asked Bill.

"Sure did. They are lying back there next to the big oak tree."

"Here. Take my knife and skin them. We can use their hides."

Tom reached out and took Bill's knife. He turned around and went back into the woods. He skinned the raccoons and washed their hides and his hands in the small stream nearby. Then he picked up his gun and with the pelts headed toward home. Bill rushed home with the wounded dog. Ma helped him put some salve on the wounds, and then they wrapped the dog in some white cloth. She keeps all the clean white cloth for such an occasion as this. On the farm, someone or an animal was always getting hurt.

———◆———

In the next few weeks, Bill spent as much time as he could helping to care for the little heifer. The hound dog was mending well and was able to walk about, but wasn't ready to go on a hunt just yet. He was trying to stay busy to keep his mind off Ollie. The days and weeks moved at a snail's pace for him. The next few weeks seemed like months. He thought the first Sunday of the month would never arrive. However, it finally came. He didn't wait to ride in the wagon with his Pa and Ma. He lit out, right after breakfast, walking to church. He put on the best pair of overalls he had with the bleached white shirt his Ma had washed for him. Then he scrubbed as much dirt off his brogans as he could.

He wanted to be the first one at church. When he got there, he spoke to the pastor, and drew a fresh bucket of water from the well. About nine o'clock, the wagons and buggies started arriving in the churchyard. He was more nervous now than he was the last church Sunday. When he didn't see the Voyles' wagon coming down the road, he became even more nervous. He would walk to the edge of the road; look in the direction that the Voyles would be coming, and then walk back to the steps of the church.

His Ma and Pa had arrived along with most of the surrounding community. Many of the folks gathered around the Franklin's; telling them how their son had saved the Floyd's daughter, Joann, from drowning. They were saying how proud they were of Bill, and the way he showed great courage in the face of danger.

Bill kept walking out to the edge of the churchyard and back, pacing like a caged animal. Still looking up the road in the direction the Voyles should be coming. There were no sign of them.

"I'm worried," said Bill. "This isn't like the Voyles family. They are always on time. In fact, they are among the first ones here most of the time."

"Just be patient, they'll be along trekly," said Tom, as he was trying to head Mattie inside the church to meet some of the other folks.

"Everything is going to be alright son, you just wait and see," said Mattie, as she followed Tom into the church.

With all the advice given to him, none of it was helping to calm him down any. The other young girls and boys were enjoying their time at the well, while he was walking to the road and back. He finally walked down to the creek and set down a little while. Then he began to talk to the Lord about the whereabouts of the Voyles. After having a small prayer, he came back to the churchyard.

The sound of the organ playing was a call for everyone to come inside the church. Still there were no Voyles in sight. Bill could see way up the road and there was no wagon coming, at all. He had waited as long as he could, then he turned and told some of his friends, if he wasn't back before the church dinner was over, to tell his folks he would see them later at home. He headed out, going up the road toward the Voyles' farm. He had locked up in his heart the words Mrs. Voyles had said to him the last church day, "You can come calling anytime." Now, that was just what he was going to do.

———✦———

The Voyles lived about ten miles from the church toward Dawsonville. It didn't matter to Bill that he had already walked more than twelve miles getting to church, the distance wasn't on his mind, but Ollie was. He had walked about half way from the church toward their farm, when he saw a wagon in the middle of the road, and not a soul, not even an animal around it. It was the Voyles' wagon. The right rear wheel was missing and the wagon was sitting with the axle propped up on some rocks. He looked around and saw that the tracks from the wheel led out toward the woods. He followed the trail. As he got close to the woods, he heard laughter. He quickly recognized the voice of Ollie.

"Hello," he yelled, as he came near.

"Over here," said Ollie. "We're here, under the shade of this oak tree."

There under the shade of the tree was all the Voyles family. Ed and Jules were sweating through their Sunday meeting clothes. Ed was working on the wagon wheel, while Jules stood nearby ready to help or hand his Pa anything he needed. Ollie and her mother were sitting with their backs resting against the trunk of the big tree. They had their dresses pulled up above their knees and their bloomers were showing. Both had paper fans, swishing them back and forth, just trying to stir up some cool air. They always took their paper fans with them to church during the summer months. You didn't want to be in church without them on the warmer days.

"I waited a long time for you folks at church, but when the organ began to play, I knew there had to be something wrong. I began to worry. I knew you folks never miss church," said Bill, taking his hat off as he walked near the oak tree.

Ollie and Ma quickly stood up, pulling their dresses down.

"I'll be awhile fixing this wheel," said Ed, turning the wheel over. He took time to remove his shirt, leaving him with his under shirt on. He turned to Bill and said, "I'm going to haft to replace a broken spoke. We hit a rock buried in the ruts and it broke the spoke. This wheel took a pretty-good lick. It made all of us bounce up off our seat."

Ed was good at fixing things. He kept up all their farm equipment. He could make plow handles out of wood, shape plows from steel, and would try his hand at fixing just about anything. After Martha and Ollie stood up, you could see their bonnets hanging down their backs, and the ribbons tied around their necks. Martha said, "Well, we can spread dinner here under this tree, since we won't make it to the church in time to have dinner there. We can catch up on all the news next month. At least we'll have something new to tell them."

"Jules, you and Ollie walk Big John and Belle down to the creek for water, while I finish breaking down the wheel. I need to take out this broken spoke. Your Ma can start spreading out the dinner," said Pa.

Bill quickly spoke up, "I'll go with Ollie, if it's okay, Mr. Voyles. Jules can help you with the wheel."

"Yeah, you two go ahead, Jules can help his Ma set up a table for dinner, and I don't like much having the wheel tore down."

Jules, taking his shirt off, leaving him in his under shirt like his Pa, went back to the wagon, took off the seats and sideboards, and brought them under the tree. After looking around for a while, he found enough rocks to prop up the boards to make a table. Then he went back to get the baskets of food. Ollie and Bill made it to the creek with the horses.

"Ollie," said Bill, when you didn't show up at church this morning I got plum sick to my stomach."

"Really, you really got sick at your stomach?" she asked.

"I sure did," moving close to her, he said, "I would like to call on you sometimes, if it's alright with you."

With a sheepish smile, she replied, "I'm sure it's alright. Ma and Pa have discussed this matter with me already. Since you were invited for dinner today, I know it will be all right for you to call on me at our home."

"Hey you two, it's time to eat, come and get it," yelled Jules.

Even though they knew they had to eat, it was evident neither one was very happy about joining the rest of the family. They were enjoying each other's company too much. They tied the horses to a limb, hanging low to the ground, and headed back to the oak tree. The Sunday dinner spread was a sight to see. Ma had prepared fried chicken, corn on the cob, biscuits, cornbread, mashed potatoes, and a big jug of tea. After dinner, everyone, but Ed, helped put things away. He was busy searching in the woods, trying to find the right size of a hickory limb, that he needed to make a spoke. Bill helped Jules put the sideboards back on the wagon and place the seat boards on top.

"You want to walk back down to the creek and set awhile?" asked Bill.

"Sure," replied Ollie.

"Since you two are going down there, you can bring back the horses when you come, OK?" said Jules.

"We can do that," said Bill, walking close beside Ollie.

The creek was flowing along in a lazy sort of way. Occasionally the wind would blow across it, causing the water to make ripples, which crashed into the bank on the other side. A tree, somewhere up stream, had released one of its treasures, a leaf, and it found its way into the open water of the creek. It was flowing downstream, headed for some unknown destination. Ollie and Bill sat on the creek bank in the serenity of their surroundings and was satisfied just sitting close to each other.

"Ollie," asked Bill, after a long time of quietness, "do you like any of the other fellows at church?"

"Why do you ask this kind of question? Just last month I . . ." Ollie caught herself before she finished her sentence. She almost said, only just last month did I start to look at myself as a grown woman for the first time.

"I was just wondering. I've never liked the girls at church either. That is not what I mean. I like the girls at church, but not like I like you. Does that make any kind of sense?" asked Bill.

Laughing, Ollie said, "Yes, that's the same way I feel toward the boys."

Pa came out of the woods with a fine straight hickory limb. He spent the next few hours cutting and whittling the limb to fit the wheel. Finally, after making a few adjustments, the wheel was ready to go back on the wagon. With the help of Jules, they mounted the wheel back on, and it was good as new.

"Bring up the horses," yelled Pa.

"Ollie, I really care about you," said Bill, untying the horses.

"I care about you too," she replied, as she walked close by his side back to the wagon.

Pa and Jules hitched the horses back to the wagon. "We better be heading toward home now. I don't think we'll have any more trouble with the wheel," said Pa.

"Mind if I ride along?" asked Bill, while swapping his hat from hand to hand with his hair waving in the light breeze.

"Not at all, and I'm sure the ladies won't mind," Ed replied.

Ollie was glad he had asked her Pa to let him ride with them. The seat boards Ed had made were just long enough for two people to sit on. Bill sat down in the back of the wagon and leaned back on the seat board close to Ollie. This was heaven to him, for the closer he was to her, the happier he was.

The trip was too short for Bill, even though it took more than an hour to reach the Voyles farm. When they reached the farm, Jules with the help of Bill, unhitched the horses and took them to the corral next to the barn. Ed helped the women down from the wagon, and took the basket of leftover food to the kitchen. Martha went in and changed from her Sunday clothes to her regular weekday dress. After straighten her hair up a bit she was ready to fix supper.

"Ollie, honey, you can keep your guest company. Pa can help me with supper," said Ma. "We are going to have leftovers and maybe a little something added."

Ed laughed and said, "You've been trying to get me in the kitchen for years."

Ollie went out on the porch and sat in the porch swing. She could not keep her eyes from staring at Bill as he and Jules came walking back to the house. Bill climbed the porch steps first, then, walked over, and sat down next to her in the swing. Jules ascended the steps, took a glance at the pair, and quickly said, "If you two don't mind, I'll see if I can be of help to Ma and Pa."

Ollie quickly spoke up, "We don't mind at all, do we Bill?"

"No, no, of course not," he replied, with joy. Now he and Ollie would be alone for a little while. When Jules went into the house, Bill took Ollie by her tiny hand and said to her, "Ollie, oh Ollie, you will never know how I feel about you. Every time I saw you at church, I wanted to tell you how much I cared, but was always afraid to approach you with your family being nearby. I wasn't sure how they would feel about me talking to their only daughter."

She squeezed his hand very hard, since his hands were so much larger than hers were, she wasn't sure he would even feel the squeeze. She, too, wanted him to know she cared for him without saying it. In addition, she wasn't sure the family wasn't listening to their conversation.

"It's time to eat, you two," said Ed coming to the front door.

They got up from the swing and came inside. Bill took a moment to look around the dining area. There was more fancy stuff in this room than in his mother's dining room back home. Martha had pictures and several whatnot pieces on the wall. He took a seat next to Ollie, and Jules sat on the other side of her. After Ed said the blessing, everyone started eating and passing the food around. When he saw no one looking, Jules would lightly pull Ollie's hair. For a moment, she wasn't sure whether it was Jules or Bill pulling her hair. The next pull was harder. She knew then it wasn't Bill.

Ollie managed to kick Jules on his shin about the time he was asking for a piece of bread. "Oh, oh my," he said, trying to regain his composure, "would you please pass the bread." With everyone laughing, Jules ended his pestering of Ollie. The evening passed quickly and finally Bill said, "I must be going toward home. Pa and I have the back field to plant tomorrow."

As bad as Ollie hated to see Bill leave, she knew it was something he had to do. He excused himself to the family and she walked him to the door. He tried to touch her hand, without the rest of the family seeing him, as he walked pass her onto the porch. He put on his hat, bid them good night, and headed for home.

Chapter Five

Three weeks has now passed since Bill and Ollie first held each other's hands in the swing. During those three weeks, Bill was dealing with things the best he could. One morning he let the cow out to pasture with the mules before he had ever milked her. He had to chase her down, and get her back into the barn. One time he went to feed the hogs and caught himself fixing to pour out the hogs' feed to the chickens.

"Son," said his Pa, one morning, "You've got it bad. I thought I had it bad when I met your mother. But you've got me beat."

"I can't keep my mind from thinking about Ollie," said Bill. "I know I'm quite a bit older than her, but she is such a mature person. I just know I can make her happy if she would have me."

"You're a good young man, Bill Franklin," said Pa. "You just be yourself and tell her your heart."

"I'm scared."

"Who isn't? When I went to ask your grandpa for your mother's hand in marriage my knees wouldn't stop knocking against each other."

"You were scared? Pa, I don't believe it, you've never been scared of anything."

"Till I met your mother I wasn't. Women have a way of bringing out things in a man, good or bad," he said, with a big chuckle. "By the way son, I want to tell you how proud I am of you. What you did for the Floyd family, saving little Joann from drowning, was something else. It took courage. Not many men have that kind of courage."

"Thanks Pa," replied Bill. He had spent these past three weeks thinking about Ollie and now he had his mind made up. He was going to confront Ed and Martha about how he felt about her. He wasn't going to wait until church Sunday. That was more than a week away. He didn't believe his heart could stand the wait. When he got the morning chores done, he put on his best clothes, a denim shirt and a pair of overalls with the least amount of patches on them. With his hat cocked on his head, he headed up the road toward the Voyles' farm.

He had walked for several hours and during that time he was thinking about what he would say when he got there. He decided to stop at the church and draw himself a cool drink of water. Standing at the well, having his second dipper of water, his thoughts went back to the church day when he was able to draw Ollie a drink of water. Remembering how she looked in her new dress Martha had made for her.

"Hello Bill," was the words he heard coming from behind him. Hearing the sound of the voice so unexpectedly, it almost caused Bill to drop the dipper.

Turning around, he saw it was Pastor Mosley. "Good morning, sir," Bill replied. "I didn't know anyone was around. You took me by surprise."

"I'm sorry I scared you. I didn't mean too," said the pastor. "What are you doing here anyway?"

"Just stopping for a drink," Bill replied. "I'm on my way to see the Voyles."

"Ollie, I guess?"

"Yes sir," replied Bill. "Pastor, I wasn't expecting to see you here today, but since you are, could I talk to you about something?"

"I've got time to talk to you, Bill," replied the pastor. "I come every month, about a week before church Sunday; to make sure everything is in order for the services coming up. Most everyone helps with keeping the church clean and oil in the lamps in case we need them. I just always do a double check."

"I'm on my way to talk to Mr. and Mrs. Voyles about Ollie. I'm thinking about marriage and I'm worried to death they might not let her wed, since she is so young," he said, walking back and forth in front of the pastor.

"Have you talked to Ollie about this?" asked the pastor.

"Gosh no, I've just now got enough nerve to tell her how much I like her."

"I would suggest before confronting the Voyles about you marrying their daughter that you at least talk to Ollie about it first. She is sixteen now and she has made a very pretty woman. There are quite a few sixteen year olds marrying throughout these mountains. It's not uncommon for the younger women to get married these days. But you need to talk to her before you talk to her parents."

"Thanks pastor. I'm glad we had our little talk. I won't say a thing to the Voyles till Ollie and I have had our say. Can I help you with anything before I leave?"

"No, no, you go ahead, I can do here what needs to be done. You go ahead, and may the good Lord be with you."

———

The walk on to the Voyles' farm, from the church, took a good two, maybe, three more hours. Bill didn't mind the walk; for he knew each step he took brought him closer to Ollie. As he approached the farm, he saw her sweeping the front yard. Everyone kept their yards swept clean using brooms made out of dogwood limbs. When she saw Bill, she threw down the broom, and ran to meet him. Before they realized what was happening, they embraced each other. Embarrassed, they quickly released the hug and stepped back. For a brief moment, they could not look at each other.

"Ollie, this has been the longest three weeks of my life. I couldn't wait till next Sunday, I had to see you."

"I've missed you too," she replied.

"Ollie, I've got to ask you a question. I'm really scared to, but I got to ask it anyway."

"Don't be scared. Whatever it is, it can't be so bad that I won't have an answer for it."

"Ollie, I've only been with you one Sunday and shared it with your family, but I feel I've been with you and known you forever. Do you understand what I'm saying?"

"Yes Bill, I know what you are saying. I haven't had a good night's sleep since that Sunday. You have been in my thoughts day and night."

They embraced again. This time it was without embarrassment and without caring who might be watching them. He held her in his arms, bent down, and gently kissed her lips. This was the first time she had been kissed by a man, other, than her Pa. What joy she felt, her lips touching his. She knew he was the man; she wanted to spend the rest of her life with. They held each other's hand trying to be supportive as they headed toward the house.

"Ollie, will you marry me? I know this is sudden, and you're so young, but I can't live without knowing you'll marry me."

"Yes, yes, but Ma and Pa must say it's alright. I won't do it, if we don't get their blessings."

"Let's talk to them today, right now. They must understand, they've got to understand how much we love each other," said Bill. They entered the house and found Martha in the back room where she did most of her sewing and quilting.

"Ma, Bill and I have got to talk to you and Pa. We want to discuss something important with the both of you."

Martha had never seen her daughter so nervous and excited, not since the old sow had such a large litter of pigs a few years back.

"Hello Bill, won't you have a seat?" said Martha.

"Mrs. Voyles," said Bill, "we . . . ."

"Hold it right there Bill," said Ma, laying aside some of her quilt patterns. "Ollie can go fetch her Pa. He is plowing in the backfield today. Sit down Bill and make yourself at home, it will be a little while. Go fetch your Pa, Ollie." She was mused watching him. She remembered the day Ed had asked her Pa for her hand in marriage, how nervous he was. Martha pretty well knew with Ollie and Bill, where all this was headed.

Ollie didn't hesitate; she raced out of the house and headed toward the backfield to find her Pa, as she stumbled a few times over the fresh plowed rows. When Ed saw her coming across the field, he stopped the horses, and tied the plow lines to the plow. Leaning against the plow, he took out of his pocket his corncob pipe and filled it with tobacco from the leather pouch he carried in the bib of his overalls. He took it everywhere with him. Lighting up his pipe, he took a few draws, while waiting for her to get to him.

"Pa, Ma wants you to come to the house," said Ollie, almost out of breath. She took the tail end of her dress and wiped the perspiration from her face. "She said to tell you it was urgent and more important than you plowing the fields today." She didn't say a word about her and Bill. She felt if she said those words to her Pa, that it was urgent, he would stop everything and come to the house.

"O.K. honey," said Pa, "I don't know what can be more important than plowing the fields, but if your Ma says to come to the house, it must be mighty important. You can stay with the horses till I go see what your Ma needs."

"Oh no, Pa, I've got to be there too," said Ollie, squirming around, trying not to look straight into his eyes.

"What have you done little girl?" he asked, unhitching the horses.

"Nothing, I've done nothing." She knew now, she had to tell her Pa, that Bill was at the house waiting to talk to them.

"Pa, Bill is at the house waiting to talk to you and Ma, that's why Ma sent for you."

"Well, let's not keep them waiting," stooping down, he lifted Ollie upon Big John. Ed led the horse out of the field and headed toward the house.

When he got to the barn, he tied the horse to the fence, and lifted Ollie off Big John and set her down.

Bill was so nervous being there alone with Martha, but tried to make conversation as good as he could. "Might rain," he said.

"It might," Martha replied.

It was several minutes before he said, "It might not."

"It might not," she answered.

Bill heard footsteps on the porch and was so relieved. He quickly stood up with his hat in his hands. It seemed like an eternity had passed since Ollie went after her father, and he was running out of things to say.

"What's this all about?" asked Ed, entering the house. Ollie was right behind him, looking at Bill standing there with his hat in his hands. He was trying desperately not to rub his shoes together. Something he did every time he got nervous.

"Bill and Ollie wants to talk to both of us, but before we start, let me fix us something to drink," said Ma.

"That sounds like a good idea. I shore could use something," Ed replied.

Bill wanted to get it said about Ollie and him, but he knew he had to wait until they were ready to talk. He kept rubbing his shoes together and never took his eyes off Ollie as she stood close to her Pa. She was twisting her hands together, because she was so nervous. Bill showed his nervousness by rubbing his shoes together. They walked to the kitchen table and sat down, each one eying the other. It took Martha a few minutes to get it all together. However, to Bill and Ollie it seemed to take all day. She poured tea for everyone and then sat down close to Ed.

With a bit of hesitation, Bill began to speak. "Mr. Voyles, I know this is very sudden and you folks don't know me very well, but I've been in love with your daughter for several years. I never approached her because she was so young, but I loved her from a distance just the same. I want you and Mrs. Voyles to know that even though Ollie and I have never dated or courted each other, I love her as if we had courted for years. I want her to be my wife." He couldn't keep from rubbing his brogans together underneath the table. He just hoped they didn't notice it.

Ollie blushing, heard for the first time, Bill say to her family how much he loved her.

Ma getting up to pour Ed some more tea, as she said, "Bill, Ollie is our only daughter. We only want the best for her. What are your plans for her and your future?"

Now he was really getting nervous. He began to wrench his callous hands together and rub them through his hair. His skin was brown due to all the outdoor work he did on the farm. As he picked up one foot and rubbed it against the other one, he said, "Well, I don't have much. I've saved a little, but I will give my life for her. From the first time I saw her, I knew my life would never be complete without her. To me, she is an angel sent from heaven. I know there is more to marriage than just love. There is work, hard work, and there is raising a family. You have to be responsible for your family's welfare and be the head of the house. Lots of things like that. If you both would give your consent, I know, I can make her happy. Ask anybody who knows my family and me. They will tell you I am a responsible person, an honest person, someone who works hard."

"Ollie, honey, how do you feel, and what do you want? I know this is kinda sudden for you," asked Ma, remembering the talk they had on that washday awhile back.

"Ma, I have all sorts of feelings. There are times when I want to be grown up like you, and then other times I wish I could stay a young girl forever. Just a month or so ago, I said I didn't want to leave my family. I said I didn't need anyone else. However, when I see Bill, my heart races so fast I think I'm going to die. I think I would die without him. Ma, I love him. I'm willing to go where he goes and be a part of whatever he is a part of."

In a decision as serious as this one, Ed always took time to look at Martha, before he would give an answer. I think he even looked twice that day. Without ever speaking a word, just looking at each other, the nodding of their heads, they knew what the other one was thinking. Ma looked at Pa and with a twinkle in her eye, gave a nod of approval to him, releasing him to speak from his heart on the matter.

"Well Bill, looks like we're going to have two sons in the family now," Ed said, reaching out his hand to him.

Bill grabbed Ed's hand and shook it very hard. Ollie hugged her mother and with tears in her eyes said, "Ma, I hope I'm as good of a wife to Bill as you are to Pa."

"I've got to tell my folks the good news. Will it be alright for Ollie to come with me?" Bill asked.

"Yeah, it's OK, looks like she'll be with you soon anyway. Going with you now just seems the right thing to do. Yes, it is OK. Since I am home now might as well do some barn fixing and start the plowing again in the morning. You can use one of the horses and the wagon to go tell your folks."

Bill quickly hitched up the mare to the wagon and helped Ollie upon the seat. Climbing aboard the wagon, he sat as close to her as he could get. The ride would take about two and a half hours. Ollie wished it would take forever. She loved the time alone with Bill. It was a happy trip for them. He was more at ease going to break the news to his folks than he was talking to Ollie's parents, he wasn't as nervous. He had calmed down quite a bit.

All the wild flowers along the side of road looked more brilliant and dazzling than she had ever seen them. It was as if it was God's way of letting her know He was giving His blessings to her and Bill. The smell of the wild honey suckles growing close to the bridge over Little River was awesome. They paused a little while on the bridge before going on toward his folk's farm. As they sat there on the bridge, taking in the aroma of the honeysuckles, Bill put his arms around her and gently kissed her.

———◆———

Arriving at the Franklin farm, Bill tied the mare to the hitching rail, and then he helped Ollie down from the wagon. For him, lifting her out of the wagon, was just as if he had picked up a feather, she was so light. Keeping her close to his side, they went inside to break the news to his folks.

"Hello Mrs. Franklin," said Ollie, as she entered into the house.

"Good evening child," said Mattie, coming over to put her arms around her. "How are your folks? Are they all, alright?"

"Yes ma'am," she replied, wishing Bill would hurry up and tell his folks about them. He did tell his Ma that they wanted to share some good news with her and Pa.

"You two take a seat. Tom will be here in a minute," said Mattie, and they all sat down.

"Well howdy little lady," said Tom, coming in from the kitchen.

"Hello," replied Ollie. Her voice squeaked when she spoke.

Bill finally was able to talk; he told them that he had asked Ollie's folks for her hand.

Tom said, "Well son, you made a mighty good choice. She sure is a pretty little thing, and I mean it."

Mattie, rose from her chair and with tears streaming down her cheeks, took Ollie into her arms and held her tightly, saying, "Oh, honey, I'm so proud of you. I've always wanted a daughter, and now the Lord has sent me one. I'm so happy. You youngsters are going to be alright."

"What are your plans for you and the little woman?" Tom asked packing more homemade tobacco into his cob pipe.

It seemed so strange to Ollie to sit there and listen to the conversation that Bill and his Pa were having. It was all about them and their future.

"Well my first plan is to take Ollie back home. She and I will discuss our plans and then we will be able to tell everyone about them later."

"Ollie," said Mattie, hugging her and Bill, "you're the best thing that could have happened to Bill."

"Bill, take one of the mules with you and tie it to the back of the wagon, so you will have a ride home tonight," said Tom.

Bill went to the edge of the pasture, put two fingers to his lips, and made a loud whistle a couple of times. Old Ben came walking toward the barn from the lower part of the pasture. Ben was a gentle mule, and very easy to catch and put a halter on. After he tied the mule to the back of the wagon, he and Ollie said their goodbyes and headed back towards the Voyles farm. It wasn't long before the wagon was out of sight of the house and his parents, and then Ollie slid over as close to Bill as she could get.

"Ollie, you know we can't get married right away. We both need to help our families gather in their harvest this fall."

"I know Bill. It wouldn't be right to leave them to bring in the harvest by themselves. I understand."

Big John was making good time as they headed towards home. It wasn't long before they were back in sight of the church.

"Let's stop at the well and give Big John and Ben a cool drink," said Bill. "I'm sure they could use one.

"That would be nice. I could use one myself."

Bill had Big John to pull them close to the well, before he stopped the wagon. After tying the horse to the hitching post, he untied the mule, brought it around, and tied him to the hitching post too. He helped Ollie down from the wagon, and then went to the well and started drawing water for the animals. While he was watering them, she walked around in the churchyard. After the animals finished drinking, Bill drew a cool drink of water for Ollie and himself. He took her by the hand and they walked over and sat down on the steps of the church.

"Ollie, honey, I know you're young and neither one of us has had to make decisions like the ones we are going to make in the next few months. I have a vision and a goal for us. It will be hard and sometimes very difficult, but I believe we can achieve them. I want you to be a part of all the decisions we make, as we start our life together."

"I want to be with you, and stand with you in everything," said Ollie. "I've never had the opportunity to help make the kind of decisions that lie ahead of us, but I will trust you and work with you to accomplish them."

"There's a farm for sell next to Carl and Edna Green's place. It has been for sell for a few years. The bank in Dawsonville holds the mortgage on it. I've been looking at it for quite a while now. Different ones have talked to the banker about it, but so far, no one has bought it. The farm house needs a lot of loving," said Bill, laughing.

"We can share our love together with the farm," replied Ollie.

"Ollie you make things seem so simple. With you, with me, we can reach any goal we set for ourselves. We best be getting on toward your house. We don't want your folks worrying none about you."

"I know we must go, but I could sit here forever with you, listening to you talk and being part of your dreams. It's so wonderful," she said.

He helped her back on the wagon, untied Big John and the mule, and retied the mule to the back of the wagon. Bill climbed aboard himself, and then gave a light touch of the reins against Big John's backside, and the horse headed toward the Voyles' farm. Big John put a wider stride in his walk. He had made this trip so many times before; he knew he was heading home.

"My life won't be the same from now on," said Ollie. "Where I use to come home from church, change clothes and go off by myself and play house. Now I will be thinking about the real thing."

Chapter Six

"It was pretty late when you got home last night, son, everything go well? Everything alright?" asked Tom.

"Everything is alright. Everything went well," Bill replied. "Ollie and I had a lot of things to talk about. She is so young, yet, she is so mature. She has the best outlook on things. When I discussed my plans about buying the old Blankenship farm, she talked about it just like you and Ma talk about things. You know the bank is holding the note on the farm, which is next to the Green's farm. I'm going next week to see what I can work out about it. It would be a fine place for Ollie and me to start our life together."

With a few long puffs on the old pipe, Tom said, "That's a good farm. The land lays good and when old man Blankenship was able to tend it, he could raise the best corn in them bottoms of anyone around."

"I've looked at it several times. I've walked over it, I don't know how many times. I know, it needs a lot of work, but with a lot of hard work, it can be a very profitable farm. Ollie and I are willing to work hard to make it that way if we can get the bank to go along with us."

"I believe the bank will be more than happy to work out something with you about the farm. That fell'er Dayton, the president, he seems to be a fair man. The farm has been sit'en there these years just going downhill every day," said Tom, making no move to volunteer in any way to help Bill, and he asked for none.

* * *

The next few weeks Bill was busier than ever. He went to the bank in Dawsonville and he and Mr. Dayton agreed on a contract for the

Blankenship farm. Bill would farm the land on sixty, forty, shares for the first year. Of course, the bank was getting the sixty part. The bank would supply Bill and Ollie enough money to get them started with the farm for the first year. The second year they would be buying the farm. He was happy with the trade. He felt this would be a great start for them, having a place of their own, not depending on her folks or his.

The old farmhouse wasn't much to look at. It had run down terribly since Mr. Blankenship died. It had been a few years since anybody farmed the land or even lived in the house. The house had four rooms with a front and back porch. The well was on the back porch. The barn had a loft, three stables, and one corncrib. The loft was small, but it would hold enough hay for their needs. The barn was in better shape than the house. There was a small stream of water running through the property. It ran close enough to the barn so the livestock could use it for their drinking water.

When Bill wasn't helping his Ma and Pa on their farm, he spent every spare moment he had working at the old Blankenship place. The place, over grown with weeds, bushes, and small trees, kept him busy. You could hardly see the house, because of how things had grown up around it, since Mr. Blankenship passed away. When they had any spare time, Bill's father, Ed, and Jules helped him clean up around the place.

Time had slipped up on them. The long days of bringing in the harvest had a way of taking all your time and leaving you with very little else to think about. Now that the harvest was over, Ollie and Bill began to make their wedding plans.

The wedding was set for noon the first Sunday in October 1828. They didn't want to wait any longer. The preacher only came to their church once a month. The rest of the time, he was preaching at other churches in the county. Everyone in the community had an open invitation to the wedding. Even if you just heard about it, you came. Weddings were a joyful time for everyone. There would be dancing, food, and plenty of homemade drinks. Everyone would come to wish the bride and groom the best.

Martha had spent long nights cutting and sewing the wedding gown, which she made from silk cloth. She had been saving the cloth for a long time for this special occasion. Ollie looked so beautiful in the gown. Bill had managed to buy himself a new coat for the wedding.

The week before church Sunday, several of the men and women of the community took time, to help prepare the church for the wedding.

The women were good at decorating for special occasions, and were able to use what they had to make the church a welcome site for the bride and groom. In the center of the church, in front of the altar, was a narrow table on which one of the women placed a scarf trimmed in lace. The scarf was an heirloom handed down from her Grandma. Another woman brought homemade candles, with candleholders, and placed them on the table for the bride and groom to light during the wedding ceremony. One of the men made some wooden candleholders and mounted them to the wall near the altar.

The first Sunday in October finally arrived. The church was over flowing with people. In the churchyard, buggies and wagons were parked everywhere. Some rode their mules and horses bare back. Everyone dressed up for the occasion; they wore the best they had. For many, it was patched overalls with holes worn out in their coats and sweaters. No one even noticed, or gave it a second thought. They were all there for the wedding. They came to honor and give best wishes to little Ollie and Bill.

The organist played very softly as Pastor Mosley, Bill, and Jules took their place at the altar in the front of the church. The organist struck the chord for the wedding march and all the people stood up and looked to the back of the church. As the organist continued to play, the doors of the church opened. There came Ollie, looking like an angel from heaven, walking slowly down the aisle, holding onto her father's arm. Ed had on his best brogans and looked real fine in his denim overalls and white handmade shirt. He was so nervous that he was actually holding on to Ollie for support. He gave her hand to Bill; then took his seat next to Martha. It was all Bill could do to keep both feet on the floor. He wanted to rub his shoes against each other so badly that his legs trembled.

Pastor Mosley's words were pure and simple, as he guided Bill and Ollie through their vows. When the ceremony was over, they turned to face the congregation. The pastor proclaimed them husband and wife, and told Bill he could kiss his bride. All the people in the church came around to shake hands and give hugs as they gave their blessings to the young couple for a long and happy life. When they went out into the churchyard, everyone threw rice at them.

Tom brought one of his one-horse wagons to church and gave it to them for a wedding present. He also let them use one of his mules to take the wagon home. The people came prepared to bless the young couple. The men filled the wagon with items they had brought, such as lanterns, lamps, wooden benches, axes, hoes, shovels and many farm implements. The women brought dishes, quilts, sheets, and cooking utensils.

At the sound of the banjo playing, the bride and groom knew it was time to dance their first dance as husband and wife. The rest of the men picked a partner and joined in the celebration. Everyone, from the young adults to the children, was enjoying the dance. The women had packed plenty of food for the reception and after the dance was over, they made one big spread of delicious food. Some of the men had brought several jugs of their home made brew and wine. By the middle of the evening, everyone was really having a wonderful time.

After everything was over Jules headed to Bill and Ollie's farm, with the wagon loaded with all the items the church folks had given the newlyweds. Leaving the wagon with all the items still on it, Jules unhitched the mule and rode it back to Mr. and Mrs. Franklin's farm. From there, he walked the rest of the way home. Ed had brought his horse, Belle, and a wagon for Bill and Ollie to use for their honeymoon. Jules had put a new homemade quilt on the seat board and made a wreath of flowers for the horse to wear around her neck. Bill helped Ollie up on the seat then pulled himself up, and with a great big wave of his arms; they said goodbye to the folks at church. He sat close to Ollie and put his arm around his new bride, kissed her, and with the next breath, said to Belle, "Giddy up, it's time for us to go home."

<hr>

Even though the ride to the farm was long, they didn't mind it at all. This was their first journey together as man and wife and they were enjoying every bit of it. The bumps and ruts in the road wasn't any distraction for the two of them. They were caught up in a realm, where all that mattered was they had each other. It was late in the evening when the wagon pulled into the yard.

Jules had left the wagon parked near the porch, with all the wedding gifts still on it. Ollie was now wondering how she was going to set up housekeeping. Bill hopped off the wagon, raised his arms, and lifted her down from the seat board. He held her in his arms, walked up the steps, and carried her into the house. He kissed her and set her down.

"Well honey, we're home, what do you think of it?"

She looked around. She saw cracks in the floor and in the walls. The evening sunlight streaming through the roof kinda lit up the room where she stood. Nevertheless, she replied to Bill, "its fine, just fine." It was nothing like the bedroom she was use to back home, but this was her home now and she and Bill would make it their home.

"I'm going to unhitch Belle and put her in the pasture, and then we can unload the wagon, OK?"

"OK," she replied.

While Bill was taking the horse to the pasture, Ollie took her bag from the wagon. She changed from her wedding gown to her everyday clothes. As she folded the gown, she held it close to her and caressed it. She could feel all the warmth and love from her mother. She knew all the hard work she had put into making the gown. After putting the gown away, she started to unload the wagon.

It didn't take Bill long to put Belle in the pasture, then he returned to help Ollie with getting all the gifts out of the wagon. He took off his new coat and hung it on a nail, along with his shirt. She stood there for a moment and gazed at the man before her. He was strong and his muscles showed through the long johns he was wearing. She was pleased at what she was seeing.

It was getting late and the sun had set behind the hills. Darkness had covered the earth. They were having trouble finding the oil for the lanterns and lamps.

"Let's just make a pallet on the floor," said Bill, "we'll locate all the stuff tomorrow."

"I think your right. There's no telling where we put the oil."

The pallet on the floor reminded Ollie of the many times she had given up her bed for company when they came to visit her folks. They prepared for bed completely in the dark. As they lay down, he took her in his arms and said, "Ollie, I love you, I love you with all my heart and soul."

"I love you too, Bill. Everything is all right. We'll do just fine making this our home." She kissed Bill and moved closer to him. The touch of his hands caressing her body brought an excitement to her she had never felt before. She felt safe and secure in the arms of her Bill, as she felt all the muscles, she had seen earlier, when he took off his shirt.

⟞✦⟝

The morning came with the rising of the sun all around them. Bill was the first one to awake; Ollie was sleeping tucked under his arms. He gently kissed her on her neck as she turned over to face him.

"Good morning," she said.

"It is a good morning," he replied. "I could stay here forever," holding her close to him.

"Me too, but we've got lots to do today." She sat up on the pallet and looked all around her. She saw all the things she and Bill had taken from the wagon. They were scattered throughout the four rooms of the house.

As he helped her up, he said, "This is a wonderful morning just having you here, a place of our own, even if we do have to share it with the bank." They started unpacking and finally found a place for everything.

"How are we going to cook?" asked Ollie, walking into the kitchen. "There's no stove."

"The bank is going to let us have enough money to get started," Bill replied. "We will go into town, to the bank, after we take your folk's horse and wagon back home. While we are at your folks, I want to see if Jules could help us clean out the well. But right now, I've got to get busy and make sure the fireplace is ready for cooking a meal." He hoped the birds and animals hadn't built themselves a home in the chimney. He and the men, who came to help, had spent all their time working outside the house trying to make it presentable. Therefore, most things inside the house went undone. It took Bill the best part of an hour cleaning and raking out the debris left in the chimney by the animals and birds. Whoever built the chimney had installed two eyehooks in the fireplace, one on each side for hanging pots for cooking and keeping things warm. An iron rod ran across the middle of the fireplace so you could adjust the pots to cook food that required different temperatures. Finally, after a long time, he got a fire going.

While he was working on the fireplace, Ollie found the coffee pot and fixed it with water and coffee. She brought the coffee pot to the fireplace and left it with Bill, and then she went looking for other cookware. After the fire started blazing and getting hot, he hung up the coffee pot on one of the eyehooks.

When she managed to find the cookware, she started some hoecakes made out of flour and some seasoning. Putting her mixed dough in a greased skillet, she placed it on some hot coals on the left side of the fireplace. She scrambled up some eggs in a wooden bowl. She found the bowl in a box among the gifts the folks at church had given to them. She put some lard in the iron frying pan and heated it on the hot coals. When the pan got hot, she poured in the eggs and kept them stirred until they were finished cooking. They were glad they had thought to bring drinking water with them. Ollie's Pa had filled several gallon jugs with water from their well and Tom had filled a large five-gallon churn from their farm. The only problem with the churn was every time Jules hit a rough spot in the road it splash water out the top.

Bill knew one of the first things he had to do was make sure the water in the well was suitable for drinking. It had been three maybe four years since anyone used the water for anything. They needed to take all the water out of the well, and then cleaned out the bottom by digging it a little deeper. This job was more than they could do by themselves. He would need at least one more person. He had already made up his mind to see if Jules could assist him with the well, as soon as he could spare the time. In the meantime, he could carry water from the spring. This spring headed up near the barn, and created a small stream, which flowed through the biggest part of their farmland.

After breakfast, Ollie and Bill began their first day of working together as husband and wife.

"Do you want me to fix a shelf for the lamp to sit on till we can do better?" Bill asked.

It was so strange to her to be involved in making decisions about things, as simple as where to put a shelf.

"That would be great, maybe two of them. One close to the front door and maybe one in the kitchen," she replied.

Bill was busy making the shelves, while Ollie made a place in the kitchen to hang the pots and pans. It was fun and they both were excited just to be together. They were beginning their marriage, by asking each other about simple little things, and then together making the decision about what to do. The week passed quickly, and Monday had arrived for them to take Belle back home, and then go to Dawsonville to the bank.

They were up early and Bill took care of everything outside, while Ollie prepared breakfast. As they sat down together, he said a humble word of Grace. "Lord we thank you for all your many blessings, and I want to especially thank you for Ollie being here with me, so we can share the rest our lives together. Amen"

"Amen," replied Ollie, squeezing his hand. As she took care of the things in the kitchen, Bill hitched up Belle to the wagon and they headed out to Ollie's parents place. Jules was the first one to meet them as they pulled into the yard.

"How's my little sister doing today?" Jules asked, as he helped her down from the wagon.

Ollie hugged him and replied, "We're doing just fine."

He couldn't resist pulling Ollie's braids, as she released her hug, and let him go. She laughed with a heart of joy, thinking how many times he had done that in the past.

"Good to see you Jules. I want to thank you for helping us out, by taking the wagon loaded with the wedding gifts, the folks gave us, to the house," said Bill.

"It was nothing, glad to help," he replied. "I thank Pa is planning on working me to death since Ollie left. He thinks I'm supposed to do my work and all the work she used to do. It's a good thing we had most of the harvest gathered before she left." He said all of that with a smile.

Ollie left the men standing there talking and headed for the house. Before she even reached the porch, Martha was already there waiting with her arms stretched out to give her a warm hug.

"Honey, you look wonderful," said Ma, letting Ollie's braids slide thru her hands, as she had done so many times before. "I know you and Bill have a lot of work to do on the farm, but I want you to take care of yourself. Be careful and don't overdo it. You're still my little girl." She gave her another tight hug.

"I won't Ma. Bill does most of the hard work. He won't let me nowhere around when it comes to real hard work."

"Well that's good."

"Where's Pa?"

"He took big John to the back woods this morning. He says there is a huge oak tree, that he has found, that is straighter than any he has ever seen before. He has some fool notion about that tree, he's going to cut it down and take a stock of it over to the sawmill. Old man Poesy has set up his sawmill again, pretty close to where your Pa found the tree. Your Pa wants to use the lumber from the log to build something. He's really excited about it; he is going to use Big John to drag the log over to the mill. You know your Pa. When he sets his mind to do something he won't let it go until he gets it done." Ollie knew what her Ma was talking about, when it came to following through with an idea, her Pa wouldn't let up. While she was enjoying her visit with Ma, Bill was wasting no time in talking to Jules about helping him with the well.

"I'll be there next Saturday morning early. Just have everything we need to do the job. It shouldn't take us long," said Jules.

"We are on our way to town to buy what we need for the farm. I can pick up whatever you think is needed to do the job," Bill replied.

"Be sure to get a new rope and see if you can find an extra-large bucket. We can use it for drawing the water from the well," said Jules. "Oh! Don't forget a shovel and a pick."

"There was a shovel in the wagon with the things the people from church gave us. I'll get a pick," said Bill. "I hope it is going to be alright for Ollie and me to use the buggy and Belle for the trip to town. I'm going to buy two horses, or two mules, and get another wagon from the livery stable to bring back what we buy."

"I'm sure it's okay," said Jules. "If Pa was here he would be saying the same thing."

Finishing Martha's tea and snacks, Ollie helped her Ma put things away, while Bill and Jules went outside to water Belle. They said their good byes and were on their way to town.

Chapter Seven

When they arrived in town, they were pleased and surprised, to see and to be greeted by so many of their friends from church. They were also surprised to see so many people in town. It was very crowded and all the stores were bustling with activity. Bill and Ollie had been so busy with their wedding and the farm, they plumb forgot about the big harvest celebration. It always takes place the week before Thanksgiving. Most of the merchants had decorated their stores with all sorts of things that looked like fall. They had placed shocks of corn against the walls and different sizes of pumpkins were everywhere. The old wooden sidewalks were full of baskets of apples, potatoes, and all kind of canned goods. These were placed in front of the stores. The day before the big celebration, the farmers would bring their collards, turnips, mustard greens, and onions fresh from the field to sell.

"You folks going to be coming to the big harvest celebration aren't you?" asked one of the young women standing in the crowd.

Ollie stood straight up in the wagon. She knew that voice. It was Sally Weldon. She looked all around till she spotted her standing next to her Pa. Sally had been her friend for as long as she could remember.

"Hey there," said Ollie, waving for Sally to come over. She was a very beautiful young woman with sky blue eyes and blond hair. She turned many a young man's head when she passed by. However, through the years, her heart was always yearning toward one young man, and his name was Jules Voyles.

Sally made her way through the crowd to the wagon. She reached out and took Ollie's hand saying, "I was asking if you folks were coming to the celebration?"

"We just may. Is that one of them new store bonnets you're wearing?" asked Ollie. "We're so busy and have so much to do, I'm not sure if we can spare the time."

"Sure we're coming," said Bill, putting his arm around her. "It wouldn't be fair to you if we didn't come."

Ollie squeezed his hand, as she looked up into his eyes; she gave him a smile, which said thank you without saying a word.

"Well that's just great," replied Sally. "Yep, this is one of them store bought bonnets. When I first saw it in the window, I just knew I had to have it. Do you think Jules will be coming?"

"I'm sure he will be here. As far as I can remember, my folks always made it into town for the harvest celebration. Don't tell me you are still sweet on my brother Jules?"

"I guess so. However, he never looks at me twice, when we are around each other. He seems to always find time to be busy with the men and the boys."

Bill got down out of the buggy. He came around to help Ollie down. "I'm gonna leave you two young ladies to talk while I find a place for the buggy." He took Belle by the reins, walked her over to one side of the street, and tied her to a hitching post. He shook a few hands while strolling about, looking at the things the town people had for sell and all the decorations.

"Sally, I know you are older than me, and may not take my advice, but what my Ma said to me a few months ago, I'm going to say to you. You have filled out all those flat places in your clothes. You just be here for sure for the celebration, and I will make sure that Jules notice you."

"That's so sweet of you," said Sally, giving her a warn hug.

Ollie left her and caught up with Bill. He was waiting for her just outside of the bank.

"You ladies have a good talk?" asked Bill.

"Oh yes. Would you believe Sally is still carrying a crush for my brother? She has liked him ever since they were in the third grade. Can you believe someone can like a person that long?"

"I can believe that. I have loved you as far as I can remember."

Her face turned a reddish color as she faced him and pulled him down where she could kiss him.

"I didn't know you ever looked at me. You never spoke to me, nor made any acknowledgment that you cared."

"Oh I cared alright. You were too young for me to say so, or do anything. I love you so much," said Bill, taking her by the hand, heading into the bank. "I have loved you as far as I can remember."

When they entered the bank, Mr. Dayton, the president, rising to his feet, greeted them cheerfully. "How you young folks doing now that you've had time to have a few days together as husband and wife?"

"We're doing just fine. We are here to discuss with you about the money arrangement. We are going to need money to buy some livestock, a stove and a few things like that," said Bill.

"'I've been expecting you. Have a seat," he said, moving two chairs close to his desk.

"Don't you worry about any of this; I will set up a charge account for you and the little woman. You just tell whoever you are buying from to sign these bank notes, along with your signature, and you bring the bills to me, and I will take care of it," he said handing Bill several of the bank notes. "When you are through, just bring the blank notes back to me, and I will put what you have bought on your account. I'm counting on you and the little woman to do well on the farm next year. After the harvest next year, we will settle everything. By the way, are you two coming back to town for the harvest celebration?"

"We are planning on it," said Ollie. "Bill said we weren't going to miss it."

"That's fine, just fine. The business folks are counting on it to be a good year for them, and I believe it will be too," said Mr. Dayton.

"Thank you for everything. We'll see you a little later," said Bill. "We've got lots to do before we're ready to go home." He stood up, took Ollie by her hand and they walked outside. They went strolling down the sidewalk holding hands, and feeling like they owned the whole world.

"We'll use the notes for buying two mules, or horses, a wagon, a cow, a pig and a cast iron cook stove," he said, "but we can use the money I've been saving to buy some chickens and enough lumber to build a bed, table, and a couple of benches. I might even try my hand at making you a couple of cabinets."

The General Store was the largest store in Dawsonville. The store carried just about everything you needed, except livestock. If the store didn't have what you were looking for, they would order it for you. They headed for the store. Charlie Knobs, the owner, was the first person you met when you went in. He always wanted to meet his customers first hand.

"Good morning, come on in and take a look around. Are you looking for anything in particular?" asked Charlie.

"We are going to need quite a few things," said Bill.

"Well let me get one of my sales persons to help you with all your needs," said Charlie. He motioned for one of the young sales clerk to come over, and he told the clerk to stay with them until they had bought all they needed.

"We need a stove. A good cooking stove," said Ollie. "Maybe you might even have a good used one."

"Come with me to the back of the store, I might have just what you are looking for," said the sales clerk.

When they got to the back of the store, where all the stoves were, she could hardly wait for the sales clerk to finish showing her all the different stoves. She had already spotted the one she wanted. It was much smaller than the rest, but she knew it would do for them.

"What about this one?" she asked.

"That's a very good used stove. We took it back on a trade-in just last week. The previous owner needed a much larger one. We can let you have that one half off the original price."

"Let's buy it Bill. It will do us just fine," said Ollie.

He smiled and said to the sales clerk, "We'll take it."

She took her time looking at everything in the store. This was a new experience for her. In the past, the many times she was in the store with her parents, she was always looking at the merchandise for children, and not paying any attention to what her Ma and Pa were buying. All that seemed so long ago. Today instead of looking at the new dolls or playthings available for little girls, she was now shopping for cooking stoves and items that she could use in their home. They needed things that would last for a long time and were as cheap as possible.

Bill picked out the largest bucket he could find. One with a very strong handle made on it. He asked the sales clerk about a rope. Hearing Bill ask about the rope, Mr. Knobs spoke up and asked, "What size are you thinking about?"

"I'm not sure. I'm going to use it for the well," said Bill.

"I have one, two, and three inch diameter rope. Most people use the one inch rope for drawing water from their well," said Mr. Knobs.

"Let me have a hundred feet of the one inch. What I don't need for the well, I may have need of it somewhere later."

The sales clerk measured out the rope and rolled it up for Bill, while Ollie continued to shop and look throughout the store. Even though they couldn't buy anything they didn't need, she still enjoyed looking at the different items in the store. Finishing up at the General Store, they headed for the livery stables to look at the livestock. Finally, after looking at several horses, Bill said, "I think we would be better off with a pair of mules. Don't you think so, Ollie?"

"You pick out what you think is best for us either the horses or mules, but when we look at the pigs and cows I want to pick them out," she replied.

"Okay honey, but we've got to hurry. We have lots to do and it is getting late. Do you think you can handle Belle with the buggy and follow me back home?"

"Sure. I have ridden her from the fields many times. She is gentle as a lamb. We'll do alright."

While Bill was busy buying the mules, she was busy looking at the different varieties of pigs that were for sell. She looked at several pens filled with them and finally found a small runt. When Bill showed up, she showed him the one she wanted.

"But honey, it's so small, if you're going to pick one, at least, pick the largest one in the lot." he said.

"But I want this one. I'll raise a fine hog for us with this one, you'll see."

"Oh, alright, but I'm going to pick out a good size hog for us now. We want to have meat to eat this winter. You can raise the runt for next fall. I was looking for us a cow as I was choosing the mules. We don't have time for you to go through all the stalls that are filled with cows." Then he saw the look of disappointment on her face, and he reconsidered.

He wanted so much to please her that he gave in and they walked from stall to stall. He had already made up his mind which cow he was going to buy for them, but when they came to a stall filled with mixed breed of cows, Ollie saw among them a very small heifer.

"Bill, oh Bill, I want the little heifer, that's just the one for me," she pleaded.

"I'm sorry honey, don't be too disappointed. I've been looking at another one, and I've made up my mind. We are going to buy the one that's tied to the rail."

"Why is it tied to the rail? Why isn't it in the open lot like the rest of the cows?" she asked.

"Calvin, the owner, said the cow was mixed in with a herd he bought this morning. He tied her to the rail to keep her from butting the other livestock. The previous owner said the cow could get unruly at times, but she gave plenty of milk. We need a cow that can supply us with plenty of milk. Calvin is letting me have her at half the price we would pay for the little heifer. He even threw in a wagon, at a very good discount, since we are buying the cow," said Bill.

"She scares me just watching her butt her head against the rail."

"Don't you worry any; I'll do all the milking until I get her tamed." He really didn't want to disappoint Ollie, but to him, a cow giving that much milk, made more sense than buying the little heifer. He walked Ollie back to the wagon and returned to settle the deal with Calvin about the cow. After the trading was over, he hitched the two mules to the wagon. Mr. Calvin helped him get the hog into a crate, along with the small runt pig in another crate, and then they put them in the wagon. He untied the cow from the rail, brought her to the wagon, and tied her to the back of it. All this time she was jerking and pulling trying to get away from him.

Ollie didn't argue or discuss with Bill about the cow any more, but in her heart, she still wanted the little heifer. With the mules, Bill pulled the wagon over to the General Store, and then with the help of Mr. Knobs, they loaded the chickens, the stove, and lumber into the wagon. Bill climbed into his wagon and said to her, "You be careful, we won't be able to go very fast, so if you need anything just yell." Touching the mules with the reins, they headed for home.

———◆———

Ollie, following behind in the buggy with Belle, couldn't keep her eyes off the cow. All the way home, she watched every move the cow made. Every now and then, the cow would butt the back of the wagon, as if she was trying to say she wasn't happy about where she was going. The trip home was much slower, because of the heavy load, and the cow walking behind the wagon.

"Bill, when we get to the church let's stop for a while. I could use the facilities and the animals could use a drink."

"Sure thing," replied Bill. "I could use a drink myself." He led his small caravan down the road and in a few hours, they were at the church. He pulled the mules close to the hitching rail at the side of the church. Ollie followed them into the churchyard. As soon as her buggy stopped, she didn't wait for Bill to help her down, and just as soon as her feet hit the ground, she headed for the little outhouse behind the church. He unhitched the mules and Belle and walked them down to the creek for a drink of water. It took several minutes for them to drink all they wanted. When they were through, he brought them back to the churchyard and tied them to the hitching rail.

He proceeded to untie the cow and take her for a drink. The moment, the cow knew she wasn't tied up any more; she made a running go toward the creek pulling Bill behind her. He was holding onto the rope for dear life and dug his feet into the ground trying to slow the cow down. As strong, as he was, it was no use. When they got to the bank of the creek, the cow plunged into the water taking Bill in with her. When his feet left the bank of the river, he did a tumble in the air before hitting the water headfirst. It was a good thing this all happened in the shallow part of the creek. If it had happened in the swimming hole, it could have been disastrous for both of them.

When Ollie came back around to the front of the church, she couldn't believe her eyes, there was Bill in the middle of the creek with the cow.

"What are you doing in the middle of the creek with the cow?"

He laughed. "It's not what I'm doing in the water with the cow; it's what the cow is doing in the water with me." He let the cow take her time before trying to nudge her out of the creek. Surprisingly enough, when he started walking toward the bank she followed him without any resistance. They went up the bank and headed toward the wagon without any more problems.

"Are you alright?" asked Ollie, as he was tying the cow back to the wagon.

"I'm OK. I guess she was in a big hurry to cool off in the creek." He was wringing wet. He had to make a choice whether to wear his wet clothes the rest of the way home or find some way to dry then quickly. He thought of the day he helped little Joann Floyd out of the swimming hole, and how the preacher let him use the extra clothes he kept in the church for special occasions. Maybe he could borrow them again. Bill tried both doors, the front and the back, but found them locked. That idea was soon gone.

He knew he had to do something very soon. The cow would need milking before long. The mules and horse, along with the cow, needed to be in the pasture for food and rest. Bill went to the outhouse behind the church and stripped down. After removing his brogans, he took off his shirt, pants, and long johns. He put his pants back on and now bare footed he came back to the wagon. Ollie looked at Bill with admiration. The muscles in his arms and chest revealed all the hard work he had done through the years growing up.

Bill spread his wet clothes across the sideboards of the wagon to dry. "I'll haft to go like this for a while till the clothes dry."

"That's OK," said Ollie. "I'm sorry you got wet and have no dry clothes, but it's alright."

"Down through the years, I bet there have been all kinds of stories told of things that happened in and around this church, but I bet this one would be right up there with the best of them," said Bill.

Ollie led Belle into the traces and hooked her up to her buggy, while Bill hooked up the mules to the wagon he just bought. He helped her up into the buggy and then he climbed aboard his wagon. He gave the mules a light touch of the reins and they slowly headed down the road toward the farm.

Ollie started singing an old hymn and Belle kept a steady gait following behind the cow. Her voice was ringing out the words of "In the sweet by and by." You could hear Bill with his alto voice joining in. Their singing seemed to give a livelier step to the mules and Belle. After a few hours, the cow started butting her head again against the boards in the back of the wagon. It was like a spirit driving her. Ollie wondered if she was only hurting herself, or if she wanted to hurt others also. Bill stopped the wagon and came to the back to check on the cow. He tried his best to calm her down by rubbing her head and the sides of her neck. Soon, she stopped butting the wagon and pawing her hoofs in the dirt.

"I think she will be alright now," he said. "We are within a few miles of home." He climbed back into the wagon, and again with a light touch of the reins, the mules headed down the road.

It was late when they reached the farm. The cow wasn't in the mood to butt her head against anything or paw the ground with her hoofs. The long trip from town and the episode in the creek had taken most of the fire and stamina out of her. Now, she just wanted to be milked and left alone. Bill got down from the wagon and helped Ollie from her buggy. He put his shirt and brogans back on. They unhitched the mules and Belle. He took them to the pasture and turned them loose. When he came back to the wagon, he untied the cow, and headed for the barn. He stopped long enough to let the cow drink some water from the small stream at the back of the barn. Then he tied her to the stall in the barn. Ollie turned the chickens loose in the yard, and scattered some corn, so the chickens would become acquainted with their new environment.

Bill came back to the wagon to finish unloading. It was quite an effort for him to get the crates off the wagon, the large one had the hog in it, and the small one had the runt pig in it. Finally, he managed to wiggle and pull the crates where he could slide them off the wagon. Once the crates were on the ground, Ollie was able to help drag them over to the hog pen. Bill opened the gate and turned the hog into the lot. Then he picked up the small crate and let the runt pig loose in the same lot with the hog.

"I'll get some feed for the cow and milk her while you mix up some grain and feed the pigs," said Bill, heading for the house.

"All right," she said, "but be careful with that cow, she scares me."

He went into the house, got a pail with some water in it, and headed back to the barn. It wasn't long until he returned with the pail almost filled with milk.

"How were you able to get close enough to her to milk her?"

"Well to start with, I untied her, and put her in the stall. Then I put some feed in the trough, and when she came to the trough and bent her head down to eat, I began to rub her and talk soft and slow. I eased a rope around her neck and tied her close to the wall. It wasn't too hard to wash her sack down, but it took a while to milk her. Don't worry about the cow, honey. I'll have her tame in due time. Until then, I'll do all the milking. Now that we've got the chores done, let's have a glass of the warm milk and some of your leftover hoecake."

"Good, we can sit on the front porch and relax for a while." Ollie took the milk and strained it into one of the empty gallon jugs they had used for their water. Then she poured them a glass full. Bill took the rest of the milk to the small stream, behind the barn, and put it into the water, sinking it down with some rocks. When he came back to the house, Ollie had the milk and the hoecake waiting for them. With the milk and hoecake in hand, they walked out on the porch and sat on the steps.

"This has been a very long day, hasn't it?" asked Ollie.

"Yes it has," replied Bill laughing, "but a very prosperous one. We're beginning to look like farmers sure enough."

"Would you like some syrup with your hoe-cake? I know where I put it this morning."

"No. Let's just sit here awhile and take it easy."

"Bill, why didn't you buy the little heifer? She would have given all the milk we need at this time."

"I was looking further ahead than just right now," he replied. "The man let me have the cow for half of what we would have paid for the heifer. With the money we saved, we can use it somewhere else."

"But she scares me."

"Well honey, don't you worry any. I'll have her eating out of my hand in no time."

She stopped saying anything more about the cow and put her mind on getting things together in the house. She finished her milk and hoecake and moved closer to Bill. With his back leaning against the post of the porch, he reached out and pulled her close to him. With his arms around her, and her head lying against his chest, she said, "I love you Bill Franklin."

"I love you too," rubbing her back gently with his large hands. Bill started laughing. "It's a little funny now, but it sure wasn't funny when the cow dragged me into the creek with her today."

Ollie started laughing too. "Bill, we are going to be alright out here on the farm."

"With you by my side, we can accomplish anything," he raised her head up and kissed her firmly on her lips.

She put her tiny fingers in his hair and began massaging his scalp. She said, "You know when I came back around to the front of the church today, and saw you in the creek with the cow, for a moment I was scared to death. I remembered how close you and Joann came to drowning a few months ago. I would just die, if anything happened to you."

Bill stood up, swept her into his arms, kissed her several times and said, "I love you more than life itself."

"Looks like we will have to use the pallet on the floor again tonight," said Ollie, as she kissed him again.

He didn't put her down until they were inside. They fixed the pallet on the floor, and she folded some quilts to make them a pillow. She blew out the lamp and began undressing for bed. She could hear Bill doing the same thing. He was the first one to lie down, and then she lay down beside him. She moved ever so close to him.

"I never believed that I could be so happy. You have made a new world for me," said Bill, as he held her close to him.

"I want to share that world with you," and she kissed him again.

Chapter Eight

They took the next day to get her Pa's buggy and Belle back home. Bill followed Ollie with the mules and wagon. Finally, they felt things were in some kind of order, with all the borrowed things returned to their owners. They settled in working toward putting the old farmhouse together. Bill started his week by setting up the cook stove. It took him over half a day, but finally he got it together, and they were able to cook on it. The next thing on his list was to make them a bed. He took the lumber; he had bought in town, and stacked it on the front porch. He wanted to keep it dry in case it rained before he finished using it.

Using his bow saw, he cut the lumber into the lengths he needed. With his hammer, he started framing and nailing the pieces together. When finished he had a crude looking bed. He didn't realize how complicated making a bed could be. He took some of the rope, inter-weaved it, and made a flat mattress. So now, they could put the quilts on the mattress to lie on. It was better than lying on the hardwood floor. Ollie was well pleased. Bill could do no wrong in her eyes. He set the bed in one corner of the room and she put quilts and sheets on it. She rolled up one quilt and put it at the head of the bed for a pillow. This would have to do until they could do better.

The next thing he tackled was building them a table with two benches. He also built two cabinets and erected them on the wall, one on each side of the stove. By Friday, he had finished making the furniture with the lumber. Now he was ready for Saturday, when Jules was coming to help him tackle the well.

Jules was as good as his word. He was knocking on their door at daybreak. Opening the door, Bill said," You weren't kidding were you, about getting started early?"

"Like Pa always said, 'If you got a job to do, start early, and give yourself time to rest in the evening.'" Jules had left his place a few hours before daybreak, riding Big John.

Bill had gotten up early himself. He had all the livestock fed and the cow milked, by the time Jules was knocking on their door. Ollie came from the kitchen, one hand holding onto her apron, and the other one reaching out to Jules. He took her hand, kissed her on her cheeks, and said, "Good morning little one," as he pulled lightly on her hair. Bill put Big John in the pasture with his mules and cow, while Jules talked with Ollie.

"Come on in the kitchen. I have breakfast waiting for you. Bill and I have already eaten."

"Thanks," said Jules, giving his little sister another big hug. With his arm around her, they walked into the kitchen. After Bill put Big John in the pasture, he came to the back porch and started getting things together to work on the well.

"I've missed you," said Jules, setting down at the table. How's married life?"

"It's wonderful," replied Ollie. "I never realized how much Ma was involved with all the things Pa does. Bill and I do just about everything together and it is fun."

"I'm glad you are happy," said Jules. "Everyone needs someone to share their life with, other than their own family."

"I never knew you felt like that. You never mention it."

"Well, there were times I wanted to talk to Ma and Pa about my life, how I wanted to, maybe, find someone, like you have, but I was too embarrassed to do it. I thought you were too young to understand. I was wrong. You are more mature than I will ever be," said Jules smiling.

Giving Jules a pat on his shoulder, she said, "Go ahead and enjoy your breakfast, we'll have time to talk some more, later."

Bill came in from the back porch; he was feeling good knowing that soon they would be drawing water from their own well. Carrying water from the spring was all right, but having water at the house was going to be so much better. He patted Jules on the back and set down next to him. Ollie poured him a cup of coffee while she served Jules his breakfast.

"I really appreciate you coming and giving your time to help us. We probably could have done it, but it sure would have been hard on Ollie," said Bill.

"Glad to help. I needed to see my little sister anyway," said Jules, flipping her hair as she passed by.

After Jules finished his breakfast, they headed for the back porch to start their work on the well. The housing built around the opening of the well held the windlass used for drawing up the water. The housing looked strong enough, but neither one was so sure about the windlass. It had been several years since anyone had tried to draw water from the well. The rope, on the windlass, was rotten and just hanging there. Jules took off the old rope, while Bill tied one end of the new rope to a huge rock lowering it down into the well. When the rock hit the bottom, they knew then how long to cut the rope. He cut it to the depth of the well and left a few extra feet for good measure. They wrapped the new rope around the windlass and tied it off.

Bill wound the rope around the windlass as he drew up the rock from the well. The windlass and the housing made all kind of squeaky sounds as the rock made its way to the top. Then he untied the rock and tied the rope to the bucket. On one side of the bucket, he tied some weights to the outside, where it would turn over when the bucket hit the water. This way, the bucket could fill with water. He let the bucket down in the well by turning the windlass in reverse. When the bucket hit the water, Bill gave a small tug on the rope, making the bucket turn over and fill with water. One would draw for a while and the other person would empty out the water. They kept swapping; taking turns drawing and emptying out the water until the well was finally as dry as they could get it. It took a few hours. They had to be fast in taking the water out of the well, because the well was always filling back up with water.

The bucket finally hit the bottom of the well. Jules was the first one to volunteer to go down. He brought from home, one of Big John's bellybands. He was going to use it by putting it around his waist. Jules had Bill to tie the rope to the bellyband. He tightened it up and helped himself over the housing of the well. He put his feet against the walls of the well to guide himself down. Now, he was ready for Bill to lower him down.

"Light the lantern and hand it to me," said Jules.

Bill rolled up the globe on the lantern, pulled up the wick, and lit it. Closing the globe, he handed the lantern to Jules. He was now ready to go down in the well. Slowly, Bill started unwinding the windlass. The turning of the windlass, with the weight of Jules, caused it to make all kind of squeaky noises each time the windlass rolled over. All the cracking sounds were making Jules a little nervous as he went lower into the well. Once he was near the bottom, he looked up. He saw, that whoever dug the well was very good at it. The walls were very smooth and were straight up and down.

He finally touched the bottom. By now, there were a few inches of water back in the well. Jules was having a problem trying to untie the rope with one hand, while holding the lantern with his other one. There was no place to sit the lantern down. After struggling for quite a bit, he finally got the rope untied. Jules hollered to Bill to pull up the rope and bellyband and send the bucket down with a large container to dip out the remaining water.

"I will need a wedge and hammer. I've got to hang up the lantern before I can start to work."

Bill found and old coffee can at the barn, which, probably someone had used to dip grain with, when feeding the livestock. He split a wedge from one of the short boards he had left from making their bed. Putting them in the bucket, he quickly let it down into the well. Jules took the wedge, and with the hammer, he drove the wedge into the wall of the well and hung the lantern on it. He laid the hammer aside and started dipping the water as fast as he could. Filling the bucket, he yells to Bill to pull it up. Bill quickly drew up the bucket, he held the windlass with one hand and with the other he reaches for the bucket, and sets it on the housing of the well. He quickly emptied out the water and sent the bucket back down. It took several times of filling and emptying before Jules was ready for the pick and shovel. He sent up the hammer with the last of the water. He was now ready to dig the well a little deeper.

"Send down the pick and shovel."

Bill placed the pick and shovel in the bucket and sent it down, making sure, the bucket didn't bounce off the walls, causing it to tilt, spilling out the tools on Jules. The windlass and the closure around the well were really squeaking now. When the bucket finally reached Jules, he took out the pick and shovel, and then asked Bill to draw the bucket up a ways, so he would have more room to dig.

"What does it look like down there?" yelled Bill.

"It really looks alright," replied Jules. "With a little digging, I think the well will bless you all with good water." He started digging. As soon as he would dig enough dirt to fill the bucket, he would yell for Bill to draw it up. He had filled the last bucket with dirt and Bill was drawing it up. It got about hallway up when they heard a loud cracking sound. Bill was cranking the windlass as fast as he could when it happened. With the bucket half way up the well, the handle in the windlass stripped out. The bucket of dirt came crashing down into the well. Jules quickly moved to the side, hugging the wall for dear life. The bucket brushed by him striking him on his right arm, bruising it very badly. Thank God, the lantern survived the falling bucket.

"Are you alright?" yelled Bill, looking down in the well.

"I'm hurt on my right arm, a little bit, but other than that I'm okay, thank God."

"I'll have to pull the bucket up by hand. You stay as close to the wall as you can." It took him awhile to bring up the bucket by hand, but he did it, with no further accidents. Letting the bucket back down, he told Jules to step into the bucket. Jules put one foot into the bucket, took the lantern in one hand, pulled out the wedge from the wall, and dropped it in the bucket. He held on to the rope with one hand and the lantern with the other, and then he yelled he was ready to come up. He could feel the tightening of the rope in his hand. As the rope got tighter, he could feel the moving of the bucket with his foot. However, it was no use. Bill, as strong as he was, he wasn't able to pull Jules out of the well.

"I can't do it. I can't pull you up. I will have to get one of the mules to help me."

Jules stepped out of the bucket and leaned against the wall of the well. His arm was really throbbing now, and the water was slowly creeping back into the well.

"I will have to take down the closure before pulling you up with the mule. The closure is too old and weak to try to pull you up through it," said Bill.

"The water is coming into the well pretty good. You will have to hurry or the water will be up to my knees. I'm going to send up the lantern. We don't need anything to happen to it and get oil in the water."

Bill slowly pulled up the bucket with the lantern in it. After the bucket was out of the well, he started tearing the closure off. Ollie came quickly to help. When he would loosen a board, she had her hands on it, making sure nothing fell down into the well. When the last board was removed from the closure, Ollie gave a loud praise to the Lord. She was thankful that nothing had fallen into the well, which could cause more harm to Jules. Bill wasted no time fetching the mule from the pasture.

Ollie lay down on the porch, facing into the well, with her long black hair lying beside her; she asked Jules if he was all right.

"I'm Okay. My right arm hurts, but I'll be all right. I could have helped Bill pull me out, but my arm is hurting so bad."

"Bill went to the pasture to get the mule. He will be right back." She was trying to keep Jules' mind occupied until Bill got back with the mule.

"You're going to be alright," she said.

"I know," he replied. "Things happen for a reason. Like the time Bill went into the river to save little Joann from drowning, that was a reason. It showed that Bill cared for others more than his own life."

"Do you remember the time my leg was stuck in a crack in the loft of the barn?" asked Ollie.

"Yeah, I remember. I'm the one who helped you up there. Pa would have whipped me real good, if he had known about it. Might even do it now, if he knew," said Jules, laughing.

"I was only four years old and scared to death. I just knew I was going to haft to stay up there forever. I remember you helped me down and fixed the board so it wouldn't happen again."

"You and I have had some wonderful times together, haven't we?" said Jules.

"Yes we have. I've missed you."

"I've missed you too," he said.

"Sorry to have taken so long," said Bill. "The mule wasn't ready to come to the barn. It took a little persuading."

"I've kept Jules talking, while you were gone," said Ollie, getting up from the porch.

"That's good," replied Bill. "Are you ready to get out of the well?"

"Any time," Jules replied. "The water has gotten about a foot deep already."

Bill took hold of the reins; he backed the mule close to the well. He put a collar around the mule's neck and hooked up a singletree to it. He then put the rope through the center ring of the singletree and tied it off.

"Are you ready?" yelled Bill.

"I'm ready. Let's do it," replied Jules.

"Ollie you stay close to the well opening. You yell if something goes wrong."

She moved as close as she dared to. Bill, with one hand on the reins, and the other on the mule's collar, gave a little click with his tongue, the sound made the mule perk up and step out. As the rope tightened up, he asked Ollie to check on Jules.

"How are you doing down there?" she asked.

"Just fine, keep on going. It's going just fine."

Bill walked backwards, leading the mule forward. He wanted to be looking at Ollie at all times in case he had to stop the mule quickly. Finally, he saw the top of Jules head coming out of the well. He pulled him a little further up, and then stopped the mule.

"Ollie, come and hold the reins, while I help Jules get out."

Bill was able to get his arms around Jules, and with all his strength, he pulled him up and out of the well. They both lay down on the porch. It had been a trying experience.

"I'm so sorry," said Bill, "I should have been the one down in the well."

"Nonsense," replied Jules. "Things happen for a reason. Now we can build a new closure around the well. Who knows, this may have happened to keep someone from falling into the well later."

Ollie laid the mule's reins down and ran to give Jules a big hug. "I was scared for you," she said, still hugging him.

Bill took the mule back to the pasture, while Ollie looked at Jules arm to see if she could do something for it.

"It's very black," she said, as she removed his shirt.

"We'll keep this a private matter, Okay?" said Jules. "Pa might be upset with me for getting hurt. We've lots to do to finish gathering in all the harvest."

"Whatever you say," she replied.

———◆———

For the rest of the day, the men were busy building a closure for the well, Jules, doing what he could with his injured arm. While the men were working, Ollie was busy cooking supper. It was late in the evening, when she heard the men yelling and laughing. She stopped what she was doing and came out on the porch to see why they were so jubilant. There it was. The new closure was finished, and Bill had even made her a small shelf to set a wash pan on. She joined in the laughter; and hugged them both. They joined hands, started dancing a little jig, going round and round on the porch. It still would be a day or two before they could draw water out of the well, because Bill would need to make a new windlass for it.

"Jules, would you mind watching the cornbread in the stove? I've got everything else ready. I will take care of feeding the animals, while Bill milks the cow, then we can all sit down and eat," said Ollie.

"My pleasure, little one," he replied, giving a gentle tug to her hair.

Bill took the milk bucket and headed for the barn. She had the slop ready and some grain for the chickens. She fed the pigs, and scattered the grain for the chickens as quickly as she could, then hurried back to the house. It wasn't long till Bill came in with a bucket full of warm milk. After straining the milk, they all sat down. Before they started to eat, Bill said a long prayer, thanking God for what they had accomplished. At the end of his prayer, he thanked God for blessing him with such a wonderful wife and brother-in-law. Then the men started eating like there would be no tomorrow. She had fixed a big pot of dried beans and cooked the rabbit Bill had caught in his rabbit box. She baked a pan of sweet potatoes. She took the milk, which Bill had strained and poured each a glass. They all felt at peace for all they had accomplished this day.

"I didn't know you had it in you. Why you cook as well as Ma," said Jules laughing. "But don't you tell her I said so."

Jules wanted to leave early the next morning. He wanted to catch up with his family at church and ride back home with them. Sunday morning was such a great morning for everyone. Ollie and Bill had all their chores done; breakfast was ready, and she started singing a sweet old hymn, as she waited for the men to come and sit down. Jules brought Big John out of the pasture and was ready to head for church as soon as breakfast was over. They hugged him and thanked him again for all his help. Ollie told Jules to give Ma a hug for her and tell them they would see them soon.

Chapter Nine

Bill headed for the woods with his single blade axe and bow saw. He was hoping to find a certain size oak tree. He would use the stock of it to make a new windlass for the well. After a time of searching, he finally saw a tree he knew would do the job. It was pretty round and with a lot of work; he could make it more round for the windlass. He wanted to shape it as round as he could for it had to last for many years to draw the fresh water from the well. The tree was the right size and very straight. He worked diligently cutting it down. With each swing of the axe, he praised the Lord for His blessings on him and Ollie. The tree fell, after a while, with a swishing sound of its limbs, when it hit the ground, as if to say, 'I'm honored to serve you.' He measured out the four-foot length he needed and began sawing the log. He worked hard for a while and sweat began dripping from his face and soaking his shirt. He was proud of what he had accomplished so far. Finally, he got the four-foot stock sawed off the fallen tree. He picked it up, put it on his shoulder, with his axe and bow saw in hand, he headed for home. He knew he would return later to work up the rest of the tree for firewood. They would need a lot of wood for the winter.

"I was beginning to worry about you," said Ollie, walking out to meet him. She took the saw and axe from his hand, and walked close by him. "While you rest a while, I will fix you something to eat."

Bill dropped the log close to the well, and lay down on the porch. He stretched out his back and arms hoping to relax his muscles. Ollie brought him a wedge of cornbread, a bowl of beans, and a glass of milk. He rose up, swung his legs off the porch, and took the bowl of beans from her. She sat down next to him holding his bread and milk. Holding the bowl in one hand, putting the other arm around Ollie, he thanked the good

Lord for all he had blessed them with, including the meal he was about to receive.

After the meal, Bill took a little time resting against the post of the porch, it had become his favorite place to sit and rest. In a little while, he got up, and started shaping up the log. He worked the rest of the evening shaping it as good as he could. It was now ready for the handle to go in it.

"I think I will wait till tomorrow to finish up the windlass. By the time we get through doing our chores, it will be dark. If you will bring me the milk pail with some water in it, I will go milk the cow," said Bill.

Ollie hastened to fetch the pail, she was glad he had decided to wait until tomorrow to finish the windlass. She knew her Bill had worked extra hard today and he needed to rest. While he was milking the cow, she fed the hogs and chickens. They finished the chores about the same time and wound up in the kitchen together.

"Would you like for me to fix something else for you to eat?" She asked.

"No, I'm alright. I'm going to get a bath in the stream near the barn. I will be back in a little while."

"While you are bathing in the stream, I will get my bath here in the kitchen," she replied.

It was late by the time they finished bathing. They got in bed, and Ollie snuggled as close to Bill as she could get. She had chill bumps running over her body. He drew her close to him, making sure she was warm and safe.

As the sun rose over the hills, bringing in the beginning of a brand new day, Bill and Ollie had already taken advantage of its early light. They were finished with their chores of feeding the animals and milking the cow. After they ate breakfast, Bill was anxious to start working on the well. Holding hands as they went outside, he couldn't keep from kissing her, before he started to work.

He had taken the steel handle and the steel rod from the old windlass to use on the new one. He sharpened the flat end of the handle and the flat end of the rod some more, making it easier to drive them into the log. Standing the log on its end, he had Ollie to hold it, to keep it from falling over. He lined up the handle to the center of the windlass as good as he could. With a hammer, he started tapping the handle into the center of the log. After he had the handle lined up and going in the right direction, he took the sledgehammer and finished driving it into the log. Now, the next task was going to be much harder. He laid the log on the porch. He centered up the end as best as he could, and with a hand auger, he drilled a small hole in the end, just enough to get the rod started into the log.

With Ollie sitting on the log, trying to keep it still, Bill took the sledgehammer and started driving the rod into the log. With each swing of the hammer, she had to readjust herself. Every time he hit the rod with the hammer, the force lifted her up off the log. Finally, it was finished. She was so happy to get up and off the log. She didn't say anything to Bill, but her bottom had gotten pretty sore from all the jolting and bumping.

"We'll attach it to the well after dinner, let's quit for now," said Bill, looking at Ollie. He knew she had taken a beating trying to hold the log down.

"That would be great," replied Ollie, rubbing her bottom.

"I need to check on the pasture fence on the back side. I'll do that while you work on getting dinner ready."

Ollie headed to the kitchen, still rubbing her bottom. Bill filled his pockets with nails, a hammer and pliers, and then headed toward the backside of the pasture. Some of the fence was down, and it took him a little longer to repair it than he had anticipated. By the time, he returned home, she had dinner on the table and it was getting cold.

"I'm sorry dear, but the fence needed fixing badly. I don't know how it got torn down, but I needed to get it back up before we were out hunting for our livestock."

"I knew it had to be something important to keep you away from a hot dinner."

"Again, let's wait till in the morning to start back on the well. It will be milking time soon and we can finish the well tomorrow. Okay?"

Rubbing her bottom again, she replied, "It sounds good to me."

The next morning they were busy as they could be. Ollie was fixing breakfast, while Bill was milking the cow. When breakfast was over and all the chores were finished, he set himself to finish the work on the well. He rounded out a place on each side of the closure for the windlass to sit on. Then he picked up the windlass and placed it on the closure, secured it by nailing down a thick plank across each end of it. Turning the windlass several times, he wanted to make sure it would turn freely without binding. Everything was now ready for the rope to go around the windlass. He dropped the bucket into the well and let it down by hand. After the bucket filled with water, he let it sit on the bottom of the well. This way he would know the exact length of the rope that he would need. He then tied off the rope and started drawing up the bucket, which had filled with water. Ollie came out on the porch in time to watch him draw up their first bucket of water.

Bill reached out, took the bucket of water, and sat it down on the closure. He grabbed Ollie, kissed her several times, and they began to dance around and around, singing and praising the Lord for His goodness to them. After their time of praise, Bill got busy drawing the water from the well. He wanted to be sure to draw out all the water that had come back into in the well, after Jules had been down in it working and digging. It was always the custom to draw out as much as you could after someone had cleaned the well out. You wanted to make sure the water was suitable for drinking.

———◆———

Bill and Ollie were blessed in a way, because it hadn't rained, since they moved into the farmhouse. Now that the well was finished, he would concentrate on repairing the roof. She was a great help to him as he worked on the roof. He carried the shingles up and stacked them on the roof and she was right up there with him. When he removed an old shingle, she was there to hand him a new one. It took most of the week to repair the roof with all the other chores they had to do. It was finally completed. Now they would have a dry house. When the work on the roof was completed, they sat down on the ridge of the roof, holding hands, and Ollie said, "I love you Bill Franklin."

Letting go of her hands, he took her in his arms, and kissed her very gently. "I love you so much. You're my life."

They sat there on the roof a long time. Finally, Ollie said, "are we still going to the celebration tomorrow? If so, we had better get down, it is getting late. While I fix supper, you can take care of the chores. I will feed the pig after supper." She was making a fine hog out of the little runt pig.

"Yes, we are still going to town tomorrow. I wouldn't miss it for anything. Don't you worry any; I'll take care of everything. You have been a great help for me to day. I couldn't have done it without you."

She was pleased to hear his words of praise. She wanted so much to be a part of his life in all the things they did.

———✦———

It was about noon when Ollie and Bill arrived in Dawsonville. The town was booming with people. Many had come from as far away as Atlanta. There were all sorts of games and activities for the young and the old. At 3 p.m., they would have the three-legged race. This race attracted more people than any other event in town. In this race, two people would stand side by side, each having their inside legs tied together, thus making it a three-legged race. The young boys and girls would race first. Then the young adults and following them would be the seniors. Women paired off with other women of their choosing and so did the men. During the day, the men and women were busy trying to find the right partner for the race.

With the younger ones, they mainly tried to see if they could finish the race by not falling down. In addition, there was the greased pig race. It took place in a ring made out of bales of hay. The children had so much fun trying to catch the greased pig. Whoever caught the runt pig could keep it, but with the young adults and seniors, it was much different. With the young adults, whoever won first place in the three-legged race, would receive a brand new coat of their choice from the General Store. The second place winner had a choice of a small pig or goat given by the Livery Stable. The senior, who won first place in their race, received five dollars from the Dawson County Bank and a horse collar from the General Store. The second place winner had a choice of a small heifer or a small bull calf from the Livery Stable.

"Ollie, are you going to enter the race?" asked Bill.

"Maybe," she replied. "Are you thinking about it too?"

"I'm thinking about it. If I did race, who do you think would want to race with me?"

"Why don't you ask Jules to race with you? He won the children's race several years back."

"If you raced, who would you choose to race with you?" he asked.

"I was thinking about Sally. I haven't seen her or any of her family yet. It's not quite one o'clock though. I'm pretty sure they will be here."

"Ollie! Ollie!" a sound she had heard hundreds of times before. Today it was a very sweet sound to her ears. She knew the voice instantly. It was her Ma, yelling through the crowd as loud as she could. She stood up in the wagon, and spotted her Ma, Pa, and Jules, just as they were arriving in town.

Ollie was so pleased to see her Ma and Pa. She started running toward the wagon, with Bill not far behind. Pa was holding the reins of Big John tight. He didn't want the horse to make any sudden moves with so many people around. Ma was already trying to help herself down from the wagon when Ollie and Bill got there. Bill finished helping her down. Then he went around to the other side to shake hands with Ed. Martha grabbed Ollie, and hugged her so tight that she almost lost her breath.

"Oh honey I've missed you so much," said Martha.

"I've missed you too Ma," Ollie replied.

"Where's Jules?" asked Bill.

"He got out of the wagon when we first got here. He wanted to speak with the men at the livery stable. Seems they want to start a hunting team next month. They've been talking about it now for several Sundays after church. What I get out of it," said Ed, "is when anyone kills a big game, such as a deer or any other large animal; they will all share in the meat."

"Well, that's good for him next month, but we need Jules now," said Ollie, joining in their conversation. "Bill is thinking about entering the race and wants to ask Jules to partner with him."

"You gonna race?" Bill asked Ed.

"We could sure use the money," he replied.

"I know what you mean, and I could use a new winter coat."

"The five dollars sounds good too, but you got to win the race to get it," said Ed.

"That's why I was thinking about asking Jules to race with me."

"I think Jules will still be at the livery stable after he meets with the hunters. He talked with me yesterday about the race. He had in mind asking the Jones boy to race with him. They raced together last year, and came in third place. Jules was thinking, now that they had grown up a bit, they might win this year," said Ed.

"I'm going over to the General Store to look around while you men folks talk about the race," said Ollie. "Would you like to come with me Ma?"

"Yes honey that would be nice. It seems like only yesterday, when we were coming to town and I was holding your hand. Now we are holding each other's arms." They walked toward the store, arm in arm.

"I'm going to take Big John and the wagon to the back of the General Store," said Ed. "You want to come with me? I feel like the wagon will be safe there. Then we can take Big John to the livery stable."

"Sure thing, I want to catch up with Jules as soon as I can," replied Bill. "If he hasn't already got someone to race with him, maybe he would consider racing with me."

"Well, come on. We will take care of Big John and the wagon first. I think I know where we can find Jules."

Bill climbed aboard and Ed gently touched the reins to the back of Big John, as they headed for the hitching post behind the General Store. They left the wagon there, and walked Big John down to the livery stable. The men, all over town, were busy looking for places to tie up their mules and horses. They wanted to keep Main Street clear and open for all the festivities. Jules was still at the livery stable, he had joined up with a group of young men. When he saw Bill, and his Pa, he separated himself from the group, walked over and shook hands with Bill.

"How's your arm?" Bill asked him in a whisper.

"It's doing fine. Pa and Ma haven't noticed a thing," replied Jules.

"Have you found anyone to race with you yet?" asked Bill.

"I was going to race with Bobby Jones," Jules replied, "but he isn't able to race this year. He was helping his Pa shoe their mules and got his foot stepped on by one of them. Didn't break no bones, but he said he couldn't race this year."

"How about you and me running in the race?" asked Bill?

"I don't remember you ever running in the races," said Jules.

"I haven't, but it sure would be great to win this one. I could sure use a new coat."

"Then we'll race together." replied Jules. "Meet me at the starting line at the east end of town. The race will start there and end at the livery stable." As Jules started to walk away, he stepped back close to Bill and said, "When the race starts, you count off, one and two, one and two, all the way through the race. I will be counting too. This way it helps us to stay in step with each other and prevents us from falling down. If we do fall, get up as fast as you can, and start counting over again."

"Okay," said Bill, as he watched Jules stroll away toward the center of town.

———

Ollie was enjoying looking around and shopping with her Ma. This time Ma wasn't telling her to not touch anything, but was encouraging her to pick up things and look at them, even to ask the price of things.

"Ollie, are you sure you are alright? You sure have gotten thin," Ma said.

"I'm alright. We've been working twelve hours a day trying to get the house and farm in shape. Bill works so hard. He tries to make everything alright for me."

"You're not thinking about running in the three-legged race are you?"

"I would, but I don't know anyone who would want to team up with me," replied Ollie.

"Don't you worry, there are lots of young ladies, just like yourself, looking for someone to race with them," said Ma.

By now, the store was filling up, mostly with women. The men were outside, gathered in groups up and down the sidewalks. They knew three things to talk about, the weather, the family, and the harvest, not necessarily in that order. All sorts of things were going on from one end of town to the other. Different ones had set up display tables, where they could show off some of their handiwork, like quilt making to hand carving. Everyone was excited and proud to be part of the harvest celebration and to see so many of their friends. There were rabbit boxes and pick and axe handles for sell. Many people brought their wares to trade or sell down at the livery stable. There was popcorn, candy apples, cookies, and cakes for sell up and down the sidewalks.

The game booths had something for all ages, the young and the old. For two cents, you could try your skill at throwing three handmade rope rings over some wooden pegs that was stuck in a board made especially for this occasion. The board was about five feet away from the contestant. If you hit all three, you had a choice of a quart of Mrs. Green's canned apples or a pint of Mr. Elrod's homemade syrup. He cooked the syrup fresh each year.

There was an area for the bow hunters to try their skills. They shot at targets placed against bales of hay near the livestock barn. The turkey shoot was coming up right after the three-legged race. Each shooter paid a nickel for their paper target. When it was their turn to shoot, their helper placed the target on a bale of hay, which was fifty yards away. Each shooter used the same gun in firing at their target. The one, who was able to hit more in the center of their paper target, would win a large turkey and two boxes of ammunition of their choice. Three judges were there to make the final decision of who won.

Someone rang the bell at the small courthouse, which was next to the General Store. At the sound of the bell, everyone, who had signed up for the greasy pig race, knew to start gathering near the area. They had erected a square area, built out of bales of hay, for this race. Everyone enjoyed the greasy pig race. To make the pig greasy, they had rubbed pure lard all over its body. By doing this, it made it very difficult for anyone to hold on to the pig.

The small boys and girls were the first to try to catch the runt pig. The parents put old clothes on their children for this race. They knew the children would have lard all over themselves, when they finished. In this race, the boys and girls participated together. They understood the one who caught the pig could keep it or trade it for a small goat at the livery stable.

The greasy pig race was different for the adults. The pig was much larger for the women and even a larger one for the men. The prize was much more extravagant also. These races started right after the children's race was finished. The women always raced first. The winner of the women's race had a choice of a new churn or a set of frying pans, which consisted of a small, medium, and large pan. The winner of the men's race won five dollars from the bank and a new hat of their choice from the General Store.

A crowd of people was gathering around the bales of hay. The children, that were racing, were already in the ring. The man, from the livery stable, had the small pig all greased up. It was in a crate, just sitting in the center of the ring, waiting to be let out for the race. He opened the door of the crate and the race was on. The children were having the time of their lives. They were trying to grab the pig anywhere they could. One little boy had it by the ears and almost held it down, only to let the greasy, wiggly, little pig slipped out of his hands. People were laughing, jumping up and down, hollering and yelling, encouraging the children on. After the children had wiped most of the lard off the pig with their hands and clothes, one of the

Brown's daughters straddled the pig and held it until the judge declared her the winner. Then the children were cleaned up and the greasy clothes taken off. After the parents redressed them, they went to do other fun things.

Now the women, which were going to race, climbed over the bales of hay and lined up on the opposite sides of the ring. Some were wearing their men's shirt and overalls, some had on extra dresses, while others used feed sacks. The ends of the feed sacks were open, so they pulled them up and over their dresses.

A crate, with a larger pig in it, taken from the back of a wagon, was set down in the middle of the ring. Even before the race began, there were much yelling and screaming from all the people gathered around the ring. The door opened, but the pig took it's time coming out of the crate. One of the men gave a poke to the pig's backside and here it came, heading straight for the women. They scattered in every direction, screaming as loud as they could. For a while, you didn't know who was chasing whom.

The thoughts of winning the churn or the frying pans made most of the women turn around and go after the pig. One woman had a death grip on the pig's hind legs, but before the judge could call her the winner, the pig managed to kick loose. The pig was slowly wearing down, and so were the women. When the pig passed by one of the women, she grabbed it and locked her arms tightly around it. The pig, with the woman holding on, rolled over to one side and then back to the other side of the pen. She was able to hold on. When the dust settled, the judge declared her the winner. Through the crowd, the excitement was so great that many had yelled, hollered, and laughed themselves to frenzy. There wasn't much laughter left in many of them.

Now the time for the more serious race had come. The men, like the women, were there to win the prize. They didn't mind being laughed at by those watching the race. The men took the larger crate, off the wagon, and placed it in the center of the ring. Then the men, as the women had done, lined up on the opposite sides of the ring. The door opened and out came the pig. This pig didn't need any priming for it to come out of the crate. It came out, charging at every one in the ring. If anyone thought it would be a piece of cake catching this pig, they soon changed their minds. The pig was tossing the men around in the ring as if they were a bag of feed. One man had straddled the pig, and for a few moments, was riding the pig like a bucking horse. The pig threw the man against the hay bales like there was nothing to it. The women were screaming and yelling trying to encourage their men on.

Finally, the race was over, when one of the men was able to grab the pig by its nose and held on long enough to be declared a winner. Everyone was enjoying themselves and was anxiously waiting for the main event, which was to take place at three o'clock.

Chapter Ten

Martha and Ollie made their way out of the store and started to cross the main street, when Ollie spotted Sally coming from the greasy pig race. She, with her Ma right behind, managed to work their way through the crowd to her.

"Hello Sally," said Ollie, "how have you been?"

"I'm just fine. You should have seen the men chasing the pig," she answered.

"We were going to, but we got busy looking at things in the store," Ollie replied.

"Hello Mrs. Voyles," said Sally. "How have you been?"

"Very well thank you, but I miss having Ollie around. The men folks at the house only want to talk about farming, livestock, and other things that don't interest me. But I'm getting used to it."

"Sally, are you going to race this year?" asked Ollie.

"I don't know yet. It would be nice to win a new coat."

"They are nice. Ma and I were looking at the ones, the winners of the race, will receive in the store just now. I think Jules is going to race with Bill."

When Sally heard that Jules was going to race, she perked up, and asked Ollie if she was thinking about doing the race.

"I want to," she replied, "but I don't have a partner yet."

"Let's you and I race together," said Sally. Knowing if she raced with Ollie, she would be seeing Jules.

"OK, great, we will race together," Ollie, replied. She was so pleased it had worked out this way. They strolled down the sidewalk speaking to many of their friends as they passed by. Ollie was having the time of her life with her new role of being a wife. Her conversation with others had changed so much in such a short time. Martha, Ollie, and Sally found the three men they were looking for, gathered in a group, talking about the greasy pig race.

"Martha, you should have seen the race. It was the funniest one I've ever seen," said Ed.

"Ma, it was so funny," said Jules. "The pig was so strong and quick it looked like no one was going to win the race."

"Hello Jules," said Sally softly, stepping out from behind Martha.

Jules was surprised to see her, and what a pleasant surprise it was. He never took his eyes off her, while they were talking about the pig race. Ollie was pleased to see Jules paying attention to Sally.

Bill took Ollie by the hand and asked her if she was thirsty. She answered with a nod of yes.

"Would you like something to drink too?" Jules asked Sally.

"It would be nice," she replied, giving Ollie a little smile, unnoticed by Jules.

"Well, you young folks go right ahead. Martha and I are going over to the apple dunking," said Ed.

"I didn't know you were interested in apple dunking," said Martha.

"Well, I just got interested in it. Come along," Ed replied. This was his way of letting the young folks be by themselves.

———— ※ ————

Bill put his arm around Ollie and they headed for the table with all the refreshments. Jules took Sally by the arm and followed right behind them. Sally had worn her cotton dress, the one her Ma had made for her, over her denim trousers. It made it easier for her to be ready to race, if she decided to do so. All she would haft to do would be to slip off the dress. Jules was really taking the time to look her over. For the first time, he looked at her as a woman, and not just a young girl.

"Ollie, we've got to get you into some trousers, if you are not wearing any," said Sally. "You can't race with a dress on."

"I never gave it a thought about what to wear," said Ollie.

"Come on honey, if you're gonna race, we're going to get you ready for it," said Bill, taking her by the hand and heading for the General Store.

The store was still crowded with shoppers, many of them children wanting to spend the few pennies they had saved all year, just for this occasion. The store had many varieties of candy and the children were having a hard time making up their mind on which one to choose.

The time for the three-legged race to start was getting close. Bill and Ollie had to hurry to get her ready for the race. After a time of bargaining with the storeowner, about the price of a pair of trousers for Ollie, she now had to find a place to change quickly into them.

"Ah, go on in the back room where I keep the quilts and shoes and change," said Charlie, the storeowner, "no one can see you back there."

Ollie took the trousers and hurried off for the back room. Bill stood watch at the door. When she came out, he couldn't believe his eyes. She was the prettiest and the tiniest woman in town. He couldn't help but pick her up, and as he held her in his arms, he whispered in her ear how much he loved her.

The sound of the bell was a warning sign to everyone that the race would be starting at three o'clock. That was only fifteen minutes away. They hurried out of the store and headed for the east end of town. People had already lined up on both sides of the street, waiting for the race to start. Sally and Jules were already there. She had slipped off her dress and he was taking care of it for her. Sally had gotten the rope, from the judges, to tie their legs together. She was holding it in her hand, as she waited for Ollie.

"Are you sure you want to do this? You look so tiny in those trousers," said Sally.

"I hope you aren't thinking about changing your mind," Ollie replied.

"No way, you and I are going to give it our best. Come on and put your leg close to mine. By the way, which leg do you want tied with the rope?"

"I've never given that a thought either," she replied. "I just wanted to race."

"Stand still. Now walk toward me," said Sally. Ollie stepped out to go toward her. When she did, she stepped out with her right foot first.

"That's it. Come over here and put your right leg next to my left one. I will race with my left leg; we will try to always step out together."

Ollie was so excited. She was a woman, in love with all her heart with her Bill, yet, here and now, she was enjoying just being a young woman with her leg tied to her best friend. Now they were ready to begin the race. There were thirty young women signed up for the race. Inez Crow was going to race too. She had found her a partner, Liza Elrod. This made a fifteen team match up. The bell rang. All the contestants lined up on the starting line, which one of the judges had drawn in the sand. The moment the judge fired the shot into the air, the race was on. Everyone started out as fast as she could go. Even at the beginning, some were falling down and having difficulty in getting up. Others were moving down the street fairly well. Liza and Inez took the lead early.

Much shouting and cheering was going on up and down the sidewalk. Each side was encouraging their friends and loved ones on. Ollie and Sally had started out kinda slow, but now were doing much better at making their strides together. Many of the other teams were doing very well, too, at holding their own in the race. At the west end of the street, the racers had to make a turn and head back. Several teams were neck to neck as they made the turn to head back up the street. Some of the spectators were really cheering the young women on, some had old horns made out of anything and everything; they were blowing them with all the air they could muster up. Ollie and Sally were the fifth team to make the turn to head back to the east end.

"How you holding out?" asked Sally.

"I'm doing okay," replied Ollie. "I think I'm getting the hang of it now."

"When we get about half way back, we will start our run for the goal line. You just do as I say and we will be alright."

"Whatever you say, I will try to do," Ollie replied.

Inez and Lisa were leading the pack. They were at least two yards ahead of the other teams. Suddenly, for some unknown reason, Lisa and Inez went down. This caused those that were close behind them to go down too, stumbling over each other.

"This is it. We make our move now. Let your leg stretch out as far as you can and I will follow your move. If I stretch out first, you won't be able to keep up, for I stretch out farther than you, and this would cause us to go down," said Sally.

Ollie stretched out her leg as far as she could. Sally made sure she didn't step out any further than Ollie did, and they quickly began to pick up the pace. They passed Inez and Lisa as they were trying to get up and back in the race. They were trying hard not to do what Inez and Lisa had done, by falling down. Sally and Ollie were making their move toward the finish line with Inez and Lisa gaining on them with every step. All the other teams were making their move for the finish line also. It was coming down to the end. It was going to be very close. The stride Inez and Lisa had, gave them an advantage over the other racers. They were stepping out as far as they could now; trying to gain back the yardage they had lost.

Bill and Jules were standing at the finish line cheering them on. When they saw them, they were more determined than ever to be the first to cross the finish line. Inez and Lisa were really doing a good job of making up their lost time. They were gaining quickly on Ollie and Sally.

"Come on, hurry," Bill and Jules were yelling, this just kept the fire burning in Ollie and Sally for them to win the race.

The sound of the shotgun going off meant the race was over. Someone had crossed the finish line. It was Ollie and Sally. They had finished first with Inez and Lisa a very close second. Ollie and Sally fell to the ground as soon as they heard the blast of the gun. By the time, they hit the ground, Bill and Jules were there to help them up. Bill reached down and lifted Ollie up, and Jules was helping Sally up. Bill was kissing Ollie repeatedly. Jules, without a thought was hugging Sally very tight. With his arms around her, he placed a kiss on her cheek. She was so pleased he was showing her some attention. Then at the sound of the bell, the men knew it was time for them to line up for their race.

"Don't forget what I said about counting out your steps," said Jules, as he stepped to the starting line to have his leg tied to Bill's.

"I won't. I haven't thought of anything else since you told me how we were going to do the race," replied Bill. He stood still while Jules tied the rope around their legs. There were seventeen teams lined up to participate in the men's race. The men knew there would be more teams participating in their race, than there were in the women's race.

"Don't forget, if we do go down, get up as fast as you can and start the count all over," said Jules.

"I won't forget. I've been counting one and two, one and two all afternoon," Bill replied.

Ollie and Sally didn't have time to change out of their trousers. They weren't going to miss watching their men race. Jules could see his Ma and Pa in the crowd. They were standing with the Franklins. Many more people were interested in watching the men's race, than there was for the women's race. Everyone knew the men were more aggressive, than the women were, so they were there to see all of the falls, the tumbling, and sprawling the men would be doing. They were more interested in seeing all of that, than who was going to win the race. Looking to the left and to the right, Bill and Jules knew they had their work cut out for them. To the left was the winner of last year's race, Ben Long. He was in this year's race with a new partner. Next to them was Paul Crow's two boys, Ron and Lewis, each had a different partner also. Their thoughts were, they would have two chances of winning. To the right was Jacob Elrod. He came in second place last year. They did not know any of the men in the other teams. So many people had come from a great distance to be in the harvest activities this year.

At the sound of the gun, the race was set in motion. Just like in the women's race, teams were falling down, just as the race was getting started. This was causing others to fall with them. Jacob Elrod and his partner had managed to escape all the tumbling down and had taken a very good lead. Bill and Jules were setting their pace, and had a plan of how they were going to keep it all the way through, if they could. Others were doing a good job of keeping the race exciting by staying in competition with the rest of the teams. It was Jacob and his partner who reached the west end first, making their turn to start back, toward the east end.

The roar of the crowd just stimulated everyone in the race. If you were ahead or behind, someone was there cheering you on. Bill and Jules were the seventh team to make the turn to head back to the starting position. The whistling, clapping of hands, yelling, screaming, the roar of the crowd, was almost overwhelming. Two teams went down, just as they were starting back towards the finish line, and they were having a difficult time getting back up.

"This is our move," said Jules. Both men started stretching out as far as they could, each, repeating to themselves, one and two, one and two. Bill wasn't saying anything aloud, but in his mind, he was repeating one and two, one and two. They were doing all they could to catch up to Jacob and his partner. As they were getting closer and closer to the finish line, so were Bill and Jules. The two teams had left the others a good distance behind. It was coming down to Jacob and his partner and Bill and Jules.

"Hurry, hurry, hurry," was a voice recognizable to Bill in the crowd. It was his Ollie, cheering them on. He couldn't see her, but he heard her, loud and clear. This caused him to put all the strength he had left into the race. He could feel Jules doing the same. Everyone heard the blast of the shotgun. The race was over, but who won? The judges had gathered in a huddle trying to determine who crossed the finish line first. This had never happened before, having two teams tie for first place.

"We have a tie," one of the judges said. "We have never had this to happen before. I guess you two teams will haft to race again."

"Wait a minute," said Charlie Knobs, the owner of the General Store. "If it's alright with you judges and the racers, I will give each one a new coat."

"What do you men want to do?" asked one of the judges.

"If it's alright with Bill and Jules," said Jacob," my partner and I will share first place with them."

Jules quickly looked at Bill. Bill gave a nod of acceptance. They shook hands with Jacob and his partner, and they all were glad it was over. They wanted time to rest up for the dance, which was starting at six.

Ollie and Sally were right there to give praise to their men for all their effort, and for winning the race. Jules took Sally by her hand and asked if she would like to stroll about with him. Yes was her answer, they left Ollie and Bill and wandered down the street. Bill took Ollie in his arms and whispered in her ear, I heard your voice in the crowd. It was so sweet. I wanted to win the race just for you. She kissed him without any reservation.

Chapter Eleven

The crowd began milling about more going into the stores and looking at things, which was good for all the retailers. It was time for Ed and Martha to make their way to the apple-dunking booth. The tubs, filled with water, had a variety of apples floating on top. One tub was for the children, one for the women, and one for the men. The rule was, bend over and bite the apple, bring it up out of the water without using your hands. In the children's tub were small apples. They dunk just for the apple. The winner in the women's group would have a choice of a new bonnet or a new apron. Their apples were medium size. The men's tub was floating with much larger apples. Whoever was able to catch one of those apples had a choice of a new wallet or a new tobacco pouch. The children's dunking was free, but the adults had to pay two cents to dunk.

"Are you going to try your luck dunking?" Martha asked Ed.

"Might as well. The kids have already won something. I can't go home without winning something," he replied. "Are you going to try?"

"I'm not sure. I want to go to the dance tonight and I don't want to get my hair wet."

The children's tub was setting near the adults. The children had lined up all the way to the sidewalk. They were having themselves a ball. It didn't matter to them, if they got wet or not, they weren't giving up till they snagged an apple. Some of the women were giving it a go. They paid their two cents and tried their luck. Some gave up quickly, without bringing up an apple, then, there were some that were determined to get themselves a prize. Martha didn't try. She saw how wet the other women were getting their hair and decided she wouldn't dare do it.

"I'm going for it," said Ed. "I don't care if I do get wet." He paid his two cents and bent over the tub. He took a quick look and picked out the apple he thought he could put his teeth into. Each time he stuck his face in the water, the apple would move farther away. This time, when he stuck his face into the water, Martha couldn't resist it any longer. She took one hand and pushed his head plumb under the water. The onlookers started laughing and hollering, then yelled, "That's the way to do it."

Ed, took his head out of the water, shook it, tried to wipe the water off of his face, and then looked at Martha and said, "What was that all about," as he laughed with the crowd.

"I don't know what came over me," she said, laughing. "It just seemed the right thing to do at the time."

"Well, I know what the right thing to do now is." He turned toward Martha, with a different look in his eyes.

She began backing out of the dunking booth area. She knew what that look meant. She had seen it before. The day she was in the loft of the barn throwing down hay for the livestock, and as he walked through the hall, she covered him up with the hay. He chased her that day and paid her back. He caught her next to the watering trough. He held her and splashed water all over her, while she was kicking and screaming.

She started running through the crowd. Some people were cheering for Ed, while others were cheering for her. He caught her next to the courthouse. He picked her up, sat down on one of the courthouse benches, and turned her over his lap. People had gathered around to see what was going to happen next. Ed drew back his big wide hand, holding her down with the other one, as if he was going to spank her. As his hand came down to smack her bottom, he gently touched her, turned her over, and hugged her with a big bear hug saying, "I love you so much."

Loud sounds of music were coming from the center of town. Throughout the summer, all the retailers started preparing for the big harvest celebration. They had placed many four by eight boards together to make a platform for dancing. They had built them like that, so they could make the area as small or as large as the need required. All the musicians were tuning up, getting ready for the towns' big dance. Eddie Long had his fiddle; Harris Elrod had his banjo. Some musicians came from Atlanta and wanted to play with them. One had a harmonica, one had a guitar, and one had a rub board, the kind like the women use to wash clothes with. When they got their instruments tuned, the music sounded very good. The dance was going to kick off at six and it was getting pretty close to that time. The crowd was much larger than years before, so they made the dance area larger.

"Everyone get a partner and get ready to dance," said one of the callers.

Many couples had already gathered on the dance floor. By the time the music started, Ed was there with Martha holding her hand tightly.

"Want to dance?" Jules said to Sally, as they were making their way toward the dance floor.

"I'm not a good dancer, but I would love to try, with you," she said, very quietly.

"Neither am I, but we can dance what we know and fake the rest."

"I would like to find a place to take off my trousers," said Sally. "Dancing with all these clothes on would be very difficult."

"Let's go back to the General Store. That's were Ollie put on her trousers. Surely they will let you change there too."

When they got to the store they heard, "We are closing in five minutes. We are all going to the dance," Charlie was saying.

"Can Sally change her clothes somewhere?" Jules asked.

"Yes. But hurry, I want to be there when the first dance starts."

Sally went into the back room and quickly took off the trousers and put back on her dress. Leaving the store, she took the time to say thank you to Charlie. When they walked out of the store, Charlie and his employees didn't waste any time closing the door. The only thing Charlie did do was change into something he had ordered a few months back just for this year's celebration.

Jules and Sally got on the platform, facing each other, and waited for the music to start. He had borrowed a straw hat from a friend and was ready to dance. Sally had worn her ankle high boots just for dancing. Ed and Martha made their way over to them. Ed was now wearing his ten-gallon hat and cowboy boots. He had brought them to wear just for the dance. He had them stored under the seat of the wagon. After the apple dunking, he went to the wagon, and put them on. Martha let her hair down before the dance started. She looked stunning. She knew if she didn't take it down before the dance began, it would come down while they were dancing.

Ed asked Jules if he had seen Ollie and Bill after the race.

"I think we last saw them at the General Store. They were picking out the coat he had won. They'll be here; Ollie wouldn't miss the dance for anything."

———

The music started and the caller yelled, "Get your partner and the way we go, swing her around, and tap your toes." As he was calling the dance, more and more people were getting on the platform. Martha spotted Ollie and Bill in the middle of the dance floor. He was swinging her around and around and sometimes had her feet completely off the floor. They were really enjoying themselves. To everyone's surprise, Charlie Knobs and Katie McClure were really doing it up right. He had put on one of his western shirts with a red handkerchief around his neck; also, he had ordered him one of those new flat top western hats with a feather stuck in it. He had it on, and it cocked to one side of his head. Katie had on one of them new frilly dresses with all the lace at the bottom. She had ordered it through Charlie's General Store, just for the harvest celebration. Every time Charlie swung her around, the tail of her dress came up, and all could see the long-legged red bloomers she was wearing, briefly. Many from the church were very much surprised. They didn't know their organ player could dance like that. It didn't matter; all were having a wonderful time together.

After a couple hours of dancing, Bill said to Ollie, "We need to be going, the cow will haft to be milked when we get home. I'm sorry we haft to leave, but we must take care of things at home."

"That's alright, I know we must go," said Ollie, holding his hand as they walked off the dance floor.

Many others had to do the same thing. They excused themselves, said all their goodbyes, and headed for the livery stable to get their mule. It was going on eight o'clock when Ollie and Bill hitched up the mule to their wagon. It would be way after midnight when they got home. The harvest moon was shining very brightly and showing off all of God's great beauty. He helped her up on the seat board and then climbed aboard himself. With a low giddy up, the mule moved forward, taking them toward home. She moved as close to him as she could. He put his arm around her and drew her even closer.

"Did you enjoy yourself today?" he asked.

"Oh yes. Everything was just wonderful. Winning the race just put the icing on the cake."

"Do you like the coat you and Jules won?" asked Ollie.

"Yes. I picked the one with the fleece lining in it. If you get cold, you can put it on. It's in the back of the wagon," said Bill.

"I'm alright; being close to you keeps me warm enough for now."

As the mule slowly pulled the wagon down the road, Ollie began to sing softly, "Amazing grace how sweet the sound that saved a wretch like me." Bill joining in took the next line, "I once was lost but now I'm found, was blind but now I see." They hummed the rest of the song together. As they reached the bridge crossing Little River, Bill stopped the mule in the middle of the bridge. You could hear the sound of the flowing water rippling underneath them. He took her in his arms, and began to tell her, about the time he sat there, talking to himself about her.

"It was right here on this very bridge I made up my mind to marry you, if you would have me."

"Right here on this bridge you made up your mind to marry me?" asked Ollie.

"Right here, right here on this bridge, I told myself, you're gonna marry Ollie Voyles."

She squeezed his big hands and said, "I love you, let's go home."

<hr />

Jules and Sally were still dancing long after Ed and Martha decided to leave. They were becoming very fond of each other, as they spent time together during all the activities of the celebration. Jules had asked, and made it okay with the Weldon's, to ride back with them as far as he could on the main road. Then when they would get to the road, which turned off toward his home, he would walk the rest of the way.

Jack and Ethel, Sally's parents, were having a great time dancing. It had been an enjoyable harvest celebration for them too. It was close to ten, when Jack asked Sally and Jules, if they were about ready to head for home.

"Yes sir," replied Jules, even though he could have stayed all night, for he was enjoying himself so much with Sally. He knew for the Weldon's, it would take a good four hours, at least, to get home.

Ethel was still gabbing with some of the other women, when Sally came to tell her that Pa was ready to leave. Ethel bid the ladies good night, and with Sally on her heels, they made it back to the wagon. Jack was already sitting on the buckboard ready to go. Jules was standing by the wagon, ready to helped Mrs. Weldon and Sally up on the wagon seat. He took the back seat by himself.

Sally said, "Mom, Dad, if you don't mind, I'll sit back here with Jules and keep him company."

"Go ahead," said Ethel, "I'll move close to your Pa and keep him company too."

Jules was delighted that Sally had joined him on the back seat. Jack and Ethel were so engrossed in talking about all they did in town; they didn't pay any attention to Jules and Sally. They still weren't talking much, because they didn't know how or what to talk about in front of her folks. He finally got up enough courage to slip his hand over hers. She never moved her hand. She had waited a long time for Jules Voyles to notice her.

When they got to the road, where Jules would get off, he bid Jack and Ethel goodnight and asked Sally in almost a whisper, if he could call on her sometime? Sally answered him back just as quietly, "yes."

Jules stood in the middle of the road and didn't move till the wagon was out of sight. Then he walked the rest of the way home.

----◆◆◆----

The Green's son, Cody, had decided to stay home to look after things, while the rest of the family went to Dawsonville for the harvest celebration. He wasn't feeling all that well and he wasn't up to all the dancing that would be going on. His older brother and sister, Randy and Dianna, couldn't get enough of it. Every chance they got, they were dancing together around the house. Cody had agreed to ride, one of their mules, over to the Weldon's to milk their cow and feed their livestock.

"You kids ready to head home?" asked Carl and Edna.

"Yes sir," Randy replied, coming off the dance floor holding his sister's hand.

"While we hitch up the mules, Dianna, you and your mother, make sure we have everything we brought with us," said Carl.

Chapter Twelve

You could feel the November cold coming in from the mountains. Bill was now wearing his toboggan on his head, which he pulled down to cover his ears. Ollie was making plans to cover up all the flowers she had set out around the house and barn. Bill, took the mule and wagon to the woods, and spent a half-day raking up pine straw for her to use in covering up the flowers. Throughout the woods, some trees still had their leaves, which had turned to beautiful fall colors. They were still so radiant, and as the sun would shine through them, you felt like you were in some kind of enchanted forest.

He finished loading the wagon with pine straw and headed home. Ollie was on the front porch to greet him, as he pulled into the yard. He had piled the pine straw as high as he could and it still stay on the wagon.

"I've got dinner ready, if you are ready to eat," she said.

"I'm more than ready, let me unhook the mule and put him in the pasture. Then I will be right in to eat."

Ollie had put on her store bought trousers underneath her skirt and a sweater over her blouse. The heat coming from the kitchen stove felt good to her. Bill came in and took off his coat and toboggan. He washed up and took his seat at the head of the table. She came over and kissed him on his cheeks.

"Your cheeks are cold."

"I'll be warm in a minute. Just having you to love on me will warm me up quickly," he said smiling.

Ollie took only the food they were going to eat out of the pots and pans on the stove. She felt the food would stay warm much longer if she left it on the stove. They could dip out what they wanted and she would leave the rest for later. Bill took time to bless their food, thanking God again for their home and their love for each other.

"After we get your flowers covered, I will get busy cutting us up more fire wood," he said. "We'll need quite a bit to do us this winter, if it's starting to be this cold in November, we will need a lot."

They finished dinner and Ollie cleared the table. Bill took a moment to put his coat and toboggan back on. She left the dirty dishes in the pan, put her bonnet on her head, and got a heavier coat. She wanted to cover all her flowers before nightfall. With all the work Bill had to do, taking care of the cow, cutting up all the wood, working hard around the farm, she wanted to help by covering the flowers herself.

"You look like my Granny Franklin with that bonnet on," said Bill.

"Well I hope your Granny Franklin was much warmer wearing her bonnet, than I am," she said, laughing at his words.

He reached down, took Ollie in his arms and out the door he went with her. He set her down next to the wagon loaded with the pine straw. They got busy unloading the straw and covered the flowers real heavy with it. The wind was much stronger now. You could hear it whistling through the tin on the barn. When they finished covering the flowers around the house, Bill said, "Honey you go on in the house and get a fire going in the fireplace. I'll take care of the rest of the flowers. I'll haft to get the mule and hitch him up again, so I can move the wagon to the barn." Ollie was shivering and her teeth were chattering.

"I don't want to leave you out here to finish doing the rest of the work. I can cover the flowers while you milk the cow and feed the animals."

"Darling, please do as I say. You are cold to the bone. You don't need to catch a cold or maybe pneumonia. Go ahead. I can handle the rest. Crank up the fire in the fireplace; I won't be long finishing up. Put on some coffee," said Bill turning up the collar of his coat tightly around his neck.

Ollie, shaking from the cold wind, felt bad to leave Bill outside in the cold, while she would be in a warm house. She knew he was right though. She had never been this cold, ever before. He headed for the barn as she headed for the house. She took off her bonnet but left her coat on. Bill had gathered a lot of rich pine knots from the woods. They used them to get a fire going quickly. She put some of them in the fireplace and piled the wood on top. She struck a match to the rich pine and the fire started. It wasn't long before the fire was going real good. She did as Bill had asked; she fixed the coffee in the pot and hung the pot over the fire in the fireplace. She sat close to the fire trying to get warm enough for her teeth to stop chattering. She turned her feet close to the fire, trying to get the feeling back in her toes. You could feel the wind coming through the cracks in the walls of the house.

Bill got the mule from the pasture and was back at the house, he wasted no time hitching him up to the wagon. The wind had died down some, and that was making it a little easier for him to finish covering the flowers. It was almost dark when he came into the house. He took a moment to have a cup of Ollie's coffee before heading out again to milk the cow and feed the animals. She had gotten warm enough to take off her coat, but not warm enough to shed her sweater. While Bill was sitting at the table drinking his coffee, she rubbed the back of his neck, hoping she might help him to get a little warm.

"We could have waited till a warmer day to cover the flowers," she said, still rubbing his neck.

"We could have, we just didn't know the wind would bring us such cold temperatures. Anyway, we have it done. Don't you worry anymore about it," he said, getting up to get the milk pail.

"I put the pot of soup; I cooked this morning, on the fire to get it warm. We can have it with corn bread and a glass of milk when you get through."

"Sure sounds good to me. It won't take me long to get it all done. I'll feed the animals before I milk the cow, so we can have a warm glass of milk with our supper.

It was getting cold enough to start making plans for killing the hog. Ollie had raised a good size pig from the runt that she had gotten in Dawsonville. The hog, Bill had bought, was big enough for their meat during this winter. It now weighed somewhere between two fifty to three hundred pounds. The plan was to butcher the hog this coming Saturday. Bill's, Pa and Ma, were coming to help them. Hog killing days were a great day for all the farmers. It was a time to have fresh pork and good cracklings cooked out from the lard.

It was barely daylight when Tom and Mattie pulled their mule and wagon into Bill and Ollie's yard. It didn't matter to Bill and Ollie about the time; they were up and ready for the big day. Bill had milked the cow, fed the chickens, and given the runt pig a big bucket of slop. He had a fire going around the wash pot and the pot was full of water.

"Ma, have you and Pa had breakfast yet?" asked Bill, putting his arms up to help his Ma down from the wagon. "Ollie has some good gravy and biscuits on the stove."

"That sounds just fine," replied Mattie, as she thanked Bill for helping her down. "I sure wished your Pa had some of your manners, son. He did have some back there a ways, but they got lost someplace."

"I'll take the mule and put him in the pasture, maybe you can help Ollie in the kitchen," said Tom, unhitching the mule. He didn't hear what Mattie had said to Bill about his manners.

She made her way into the house, and was greeted by a big smile from Ollie, who was still at the stove trying to keep her body warm.

"Good morning child," said Mattie, "how've you been?"

"Doing just fine, how about yourself?"

"I guess I'm as good as can be except for this darn lumbago that acts up every now and then. Doc Sands gives me something for it when I see him, which is not very often. I sorter believe it is nothing else but moonshine whiskey with a little coloring in it. That's what it tastes like."

"Well come on in and sit down, I'll have breakfast ready for all of us in just a few minutes," replied Ollie.

While waiting on his Pa to take the mule to the pasture, Bill put more wood on the fire around the pot. When Tom came back from the pasture, he came over to the fire. It felt good to him as he backed his backside toward the heat and warmed his hands behind him.

"Let's go inside. I guess Ollie has everything ready for us to eat," said Bill as they made their way toward the house.

"Come on in," said Ollie. "We've been waiting for you two to get through. I've got breakfast ready." She had scrambled a pan of eggs and made some red-eye gravy from the sausage grease to go with them. By the time Tom had washed up, she had poured the coffee, and opened a jar of pear preserves, that her Ma had given to them. They all sat down and Bill asked the blessing for the food they were about to receive. In so many words, he asked the Lord to help each one of them to care more about each other.

After a good hearty breakfast, it was time to get to work. Bill and Tom went to the hog pen with Tom's rifle. He had brought it with him just for this occasion. Ollie didn't want to see it happen. As always, she had gotten too close to all the animals, and it was hard for her to let go of any of them. She knew what had to be, but she had rather not see it happen to any of them. She and Mattie cleaned up the table and put things away. The sound of the gun going off meant it was time to put all memories behind, and start to work on the hog.

Bill and Tom rolled the hog on to a sled and pulled the hog to a wooden tripod that Bill had erected close to the wash pot. After tying the hind feet of the hog together to a singletree with a rope, they pulled the hog up, having its head down. They got busy pouring the hot water over the hog and scraping off all the hair they could get to come off. When the hot water hit the cold hog, steam rose up from it, creating a small cloud around them.

Tom was good at butchering hogs. He knew how to cut one up to have the best cuts of pork. He received many invitations for him to help kill hogs each winter. As soon as they were through using the hot water, they dipped all of the remaining water out of the pot. They were going to use the same pot to cook out the trimmings to get the lard. Ollie and Mattie was now busy helping the men. Bill had made a table and a saltbox out of some of the lumber he bought in Dawsonville. When Tom would cut a part of the hog off, such as a ham or a midland, Bill would lay it on the table. Ollie and Mattie would take over, and stayed busy trimming off the fat, and putting it in the pot to cook.

Finally, the men had the hog all quartered up, and on the table. They all were now busy trimming off all the fat they could. The pot was getting hotter and hotter; the fat was cooking out real good. Every now and then, Bill or Tom would take the big wooden paddle that Bill had made, and stir the pot and take out a few cracklings to eat. As the fat cooked down to lard, Ollie was busy dipping out the cracklings and pork skins from the pot. She put them in a big pan from the kitchen.

By the end of the day, they all were glad this part was over. Bill had cut out some ham and pork chops for his parents to take home with them. It was a custom, when you went to help someone kill hogs, you shared in the bounty. They were getting ready to head towards home. Tom went to the barn, got his mule, and hitched him to the wagon. As they were saying their good-byes, Mattie hugged Ollie and said, "Ollie, I love you. You are so good for Bill. All the time he was growing up, I prayed that he would someday find a wife, and she would be good to him. He is our only child.

After he was born, the doctor told me I couldn't have any more children. I never did know the real reason; I just know I've never been able to get pregnant again."

"I love you too," said Ollie. "Bill and I are good for each other."

They watched as Tom and Mattie's wagon rolled out of sight. The day had been long and filled with hard work. He knew his parents had worked hard helping them butcher the hog for their winter meat. He only wished his Pa would remember the days he had treated his Ma with deeper respect. He didn't know what had happened through the years to cause him to change. He prayed that his Pa would recognize the hurt he was creating, and start making things better between them.

Bill waited to salt down the hams and the shoulders. He took them to the front porch and hung them up to cured for a day or two. Ollie was busy dipping the lard from the pot into tin cans. He salted down the tenderloins, fatback, and the streak-o-lean and took them, along with the cracklings into the house. He hung the loins and fatback with the streak-o-lean on the back wall of the kitchen to cure for a few days before putting them in the saltbox. After she had dipped out all the lard, she put the lid on the cans. She waited for Bill to take them into the house. They had a large pan full with scraps; they had trimmed off the hog. They knew what to do with the scraps; they would add them to the pork shoulders to make sausage.

"Do you still feel scared to milk the cow?" asked Bill.

"Yes I do," she replied. "I've watched her in the pasture trying her best to butt the mules. I've wished many times over, we had gotten the little heifer. I'm scared to death of that cow."

"She has been faithful giving us plenty of milk," he replied. "Maybe one day you will feel better about her."

"Maybe, till then, it's best you continue doing the milking."

Bill took the milk pail and headed for the barn. Ollie took some slop for the pig and some grain for the chickens. After all the chores were complete, they curled up on a pallet next to the fireplace. The first thing he knew his Ollie was sound asleep, lying wrapped up in his arms. He didn't want to move, he was afraid he would wake her. So, he just stretched his arm over to the rocker, where she had some of her quilts stacked and managed to pull one off. Then he covered them up with it. They slept there till daylight.

"I think I better go down by the river this morning and check on my rabbit boxes. I missed doing it yesterday. You think you can handle grinding up the meat while I'm gone?" He had mounted the hand meat grinder to the table where she could get to it easily.

"You go ahead. When I get through grinding up the meat, I'll season it and start cooking up the sausage. By the time you get back, I should have some ready for canning," replied Ollie.

Bill couldn't leave without hugging and kissing her bye. He padded her on her backside with a gentle hand, and left her grinding the meat. He took with him his shotgun and a tote sack. He never left the house to go into the woods without his gun. He always said, 'you never know what you might run into.' In his coat pocket were apple peelings, from the apples he had peeled this morning, before milking the cow. The peelings made good bait for his rabbit boxes. The rabbits like apple peelings. He had given the peeled apples to his mules.

He walked the trail from the house going toward the river very slowly. In the past, he had seen a deer in the distance. He was hoping he might see one close up, and maybe with a good shot, he could get them some good venison meat, for a change. When he got to the first box, the lid was down. Bill was happy; he just knew he had caught something in the box. He stood the box on its end, and slowly opened the lid. To his disappointment, there wasn't anything inside. Something had tripped the trigger causing the lid to shut. It could have been a strong wind or maybe even a bird of some kind landed on the trigger. The trigger stood up in the middle of the box. Whatever, Bill put more apple peelings in the box and reset it. He picked up the sack with his gun and headed on down toward the river. He could see deer tracks every now and then in the sandy spots on the trail. He kept his gun in a position to be able to raise it and fire quickly, if he did come close to a deer.

When he came to the second box, he was again disappointed. It was ok. The lid was open and nothing had bothered the box. He took the box and stood it on its end, and then he put some of the fresh peelings in the bottom and reset it. He moved on to his third box. He was happy to find the lid closed. He could see it from a fair distance away. He picked up his pace, anxious to see what he had trapped, if anything. He was trying not to get too excited about the lid being down, for he just had the experience of not finding anything in his first box, even though the lid was down. He laid his gun down, stood the box on its end, and slowly eased the lid open. He could tell he had caught a rabbit. He eased his hand down inside the box and worked it around until he got hold of the rabbit's hind legs. He made sure he had a good hold on it before he pulled it from the box.

The rabbit didn't make a fuss. He opened the sack and dropped the rabbit inside, tying the end together with a small rope. He took out some of the peelings and re-baited the box. This time he moved the box a little further off the trail. He reset the lid with the trigger barely attached to the holding point. He made sure not to handle the box too much. Animals had a way of telling, by smelling, if a human had been close by.

Bill was feeling much better, now that he had trapped himself a rabbit. He picked up his gun, threw the sack over his shoulders, and headed to his fourth and last box. He really did get excited when he saw the lid closed on that box. He put the gun down and laid the sack close to it. He stood the box on its end just as he did with the others. He eased the lid open and for a moment, he was scared at what he saw. There were two bright eyes, looking through two white rings at him. It was a raccoon, but much smaller than what he thought. When he realized it was only a baby raccoon, he eased his hand down inside the box. This time he made sure his hand was around the neck of the raccoon instead of its feet. He didn't know if they would bite being this small or not. It was a mystery, with it being so small, how it had gotten away from its mother. A mother raccoon was one, who made sure all her babies were close to her. She would fight until death to protect them. Yet here was one all alone in this rabbit box.

He pulled the tiny raccoon from the box and held it up to get a good look at it. Then placed it in the sack with the rabbit and re-baited the box with the rest of the apple peelings. After resetting the trigger to this box, he picked up his gun, threw the sack over his shoulder, and headed toward home.

Meanwhile, Ollie had managed to grind up all the meat. She seasoned some of it hot and left some mild. Bill liked his sausage seasoned hotter than she did. She had started cooking the milder sausage first. This way she could tell where she had gotten to with the cooking. She was pleased to hear his footsteps on the porch. Knowing now, she would have some help finishing up with the sausage.

"How is it going?" he asked, coming into the kitchen.

"Very well, how did you do?"

"Wait till I put my gun up. I want to show you something."

Her curiosity was about to get the best of her. She kept watching the sack move about on the kitchen floor. She sat aside her pan of sausage and waited until Bill untied the sack. He reached his hand down in the sack, being very careful not to let the rabbit loose. He took the tiny raccoon in one hand and held the end of the sack tightly with the other hand. Ollie's eyes opened wide when she saw the tiny creature in Bill's hand. His hands were so large, when closed the raccoon was almost hid in them.

"Where in the world did you find it?" asked Ollie, reaching out to take it from his hands. She was very careful not to squeeze it too hard. She could feel its ribs through its fur.

"It was in one of my rabbit boxes," he replied. "How it got there and where its mother is, I don't know. It seems so weak. It hasn't put up much of a fuss since I took it out of the rabbit box."

"Get me a spoon of water," said Ollie, rubbing the raccoon very gently with her hands. The raccoon was pleased to have someone to cuddle him. It never made any effort to get away from her.

Bill took one of their spoons, filled it with water, and brought it to Ollie. She sat down and put the spoon of water to the raccoon's mouth. The raccoon first sniffed at the water, then licked at it with its tongue.

"Can we keep it," she asked.

"I guess so," Bill replied, "Looks like its mother has abandoned it."

She was pleased. She handed it back to Bill, washed her hands, and went back to cooking the sausage. He put the raccoon back in the sack with the rabbit and tied it up again. While she continued to cook the sausage, he took the animals to the barn. He separated them by putting each in a different chicken coop. He came back to the kitchen, washed his hands, and helped Ollie with the canning of the sausage. She packed the jars with sausage almost to the top. Bill took the warm grease and poured it over the sausage, filling it to the top, and then sealed the jars.

"You looked so happy when you saw the little raccoon," said Bill.

"It seems so small. I just want to help it somehow."

"No wonder I love you so. You love everything."

Chapter Thirteen

Bill built a box that looked like a small house, with a large round hole in the front of it, for the raccoon to live in. Ollie brought the tiny animal into the house, where she could look after it. She took care of the raccoon as she did with all the other animals, and like all the others, she became very attached to it. Before the raccoon would eat the food she gave him, he would wash his hands in the small bowl of water that Ollie placed nearby. Watching the raccoon wash his paws before each meal taught them just how great God was. How He could put within a small tiny animal the instinct to wash its hands before it would eat. The rabbit fell to the fate of a frying pan, hot biscuits, and gravy.

Thanksgiving was coming quickly for Ollie and Bill. It was only a week away. They had been so busy working and repairing the old farmhouse, killing the hog, canning the sausage, taking care of the animals; they just forgot how close Thanksgiving was.

"Hello in there." The voice was familiar, a voice Ollie had heard so often before. She went running out to meet him. It was Jules sitting on Big John.

"Get down and stay awhile," said Bill, following Ollie out the door.

"Can't," replied Jules. "I've got to make my rounds and get home before dark. Pa wants me to help him with something."

"What in the world?" Ollie asked.

"Don't know. He just said for me to make my round and get home before dark. You know how Pa is; when he wants something done, he wants it done now. Ma and Pa wants yaw to come home for Thanksgiving."

"Oh Bill, let's go. We can have our first Thanksgiving as one big family."

"That's what Pa said. That's why I'm on my way to your folks, Bill, to invite them too."

"I can't think of anything better," Bill replied putting his arms around Ollie.

"It's best I be going," said Jules, "still a lot of miles to cover."

"Can I get you anything, something to eat, maybe something to drink?" asked Ollie.

"No thanks, but thanks anyway," he replied.

Ollie made her way around to the left side of Big John and patted Jules on his leg. He reached down and patted her hand, touching the reins to Big John; he headed toward the Franklin's farm.

"Wait! Wait a minute," said Ollie running after Jules.

Jules stopped Big John and waited for her to catch up.

"Tell Ma we will come early Thanksgiving Day to give her a hand with things."

"Just take your time coming. Sally is coming Thanksgiving Day to help Ma," said Jules, grinning from ear to ear.

"Wonderful. I'm so glad you and her are seeing each other now," said Ollie, putting her hands deep her apron pockets and twisting about.

"To tell you the truth I don't know how I missed noticing her through the years."

"Things just have a way of filling out," said Ollie, walking away with a cunning smile on her face.

From end to end on the long table, it was filled with all kinds of covered dishes with all sorts of foods and desserts. Mattie had baked two sweet potato pies and brought them, along with a quart of her special homemade relish, made from green tomatoes and hot peppers. Everyone was having a wonderful time. Ollie was telling them about her newfound friend, the raccoon, she had named him Hershel; how smart he was and how he would wash his hands before eating. Jules and Sally had managed to sit by themselves at the fireplace; Tom and Ed had stepped out on the porch with their corncob pipe to have a smoke. Mattie, Martha, and Ollie were putting the final additions to the dinner table.

Finally, everything was ready. Everyone took their place around the table, with Ed setting down at the head of the table, which was his normal place. They joined hands and bowed their heads, as Ed led them in a prayer of thanksgiving. After the prayer, Tom took his glass of tea, stood up and said, "I want to make a toast. I want to toast the Voyles family for inviting us today and giving us a daughter we never had." Tom tipped his glass, took a sip, and sat back down. Mattie amen the toast with a "here, here."

Bill stood with his hands trembling, his voice squeaking, and said, "I thank God for my Ollie, her family and mine. Also, for the wonderful brother-in-law I have."

Everyone sat quietly, listening, waiting, to see if there was anything else anyone wanted to say. After a moment of silence, Ed said, "Amen, let's eat."

The snow was falling rapidly. It looked like it might be deeper than the pastor had predicted. Every year, since he came to Dawsonville to pastor the church, on the first Sunday in November, he makes a prediction about the amount of snow we will get for the year. So far, he had been close to being right about the amount. Everyone was getting excited about the snow. It was only a few days until Christmas, and it would be wonderful, if the white fluffy snow would stay on the ground until after Christmas. Bill and Ollie stood on the porch watching the snowfall.

"It is so beautiful," said Ollie, as she held her hand out letting the snow fill her hand. She managed to make a small snowball and threw it at Bill, hitting the hat he was wearing. He picked her up and off the porch, they went. When he sat her down, he picked up some snow and covered her head with it. The snow fight was on. Back and forth the snowballs were flying, sometimes hitting their targets.

"I give up," said Bill. Knowing, if he didn't, the fight would go on forever.

"Me too," said Ollie. "It was fun."

He picked her up and sat her back on the porch. "I need to go tree hunting. It might take me awhile, but don't worry, I'll be back before dark."

She kissed him, shook the snow from her clothes, and stayed on the porch watching him go out of sight with an axe in his hand. Ollie went back inside the house where Hershel warmly greeted her. The moment she sat down, he hopped up into her lap. She took a few moments to rub his back and talk to him. He would look at her, as if he knew exactly what she was saying. It was close to dark when Bill returned. He had with him a beautiful cedar tree. He stood it on the porch and came inside. Ollie had Hershel in her lap rubbing his furry tail.

"I've got us a beautiful tree for Christmas. Where are we going to put it?" he asked.

"Let's put it in front of the window. Then we can see it while we are inside and when we are outside," she replied. Neither one was saying much about what they had each other for Christmas. He brought the tree in and placed it where she wanted it. They decorated it with strings of popcorn and a few pieces of red and white strips of cloth. When they finished decorating the tree, it was beautiful.

Ollie had started a fire in the stove. She wanted to heat up what she had cooked for their supper, while she was cooking their breakfast this morning. In addition, she wanted to bake some syrup cookies for their holiday. Bill took the milk pail and headed for the barn. The sound of the cow mooing was enough to tell him to hurry up. As he sat there milking the cow, he felt proud of himself, and how he had pulled it off, buying Ollie a Christmas gift at the harvest celebration. He had picked out for her a gold necklace with a heart shape locket. He was able to do it, while she was with Sally. Now, to get it under the tree without her knowing was going to be something else.

Ollie had been a little mischievous herself. During the time, she spent with her Ma in the General Store; she was able to pick up a pocket watch for him. Mr. Knob let her have it on credit until their first crop came in. She had wrapped it with a cloth and hid it in the meal box. She was putting a pan of the syrup cookies in the stove to bake, when Bill came in with the milk.

"You've got the place smelling good," he said, setting the milk on the table.

"You ready for supper?" she asked.

"Any time, the cow just out did herself tonight. I almost got the pail full. She has really settled down. Maybe you could try to milk her sometime."

"Maybe, but no way soon, I'm still scared of her. When I'm close to the pasture fence and she sees me she starts pawing the ground," said Ollie. Her hands began to tremble. Just the thoughts of having to one-day milk that cow, scared her to death.

"She's just playing with your mind," said Bill.

"I don't care what she's doing, I'm scared of her." She finished preparing supper, while he strained the milk. They sat down at the table and with heads bowed; they gave God the glory for all their accomplishments. Then Bill said, a quiet "Amen."

———————

Christmas Eve night had finally come to the Franklin's home. Ollie and Bill had finished all their chores and settled in for the night. They were sitting in front of the fireplace. Bill had put a few larger logs on the fire to hold it until morning.

"Just think, this is our first Christmas together. This time last year, I was sitting around the fire with Ma and Pa, watching the two of them hold hands and kiss each other, as they passed out their gifts. I was day dreaming about you, and hoping one day I would be with you, and loving you just like they were doing," said Bill.

"What were you doing this time last year?" he asked.

"I was worrying Ma and Pa to death trying to get them to tell me what I had for Christmas," said Ollie. "They always made sure that I didn't know till the last minute. Jules always had some kind of surprise for me."

"Do you miss being there with them this year?" asked Bill.

"I guess you will always have the thoughts of being with your folks at Christmas, but I wouldn't trade tonight for anything," she replied.

"It's getting late, are you about ready for bed?"

"I was about to ask you the same thing."

As usual, Bill picked her up and headed for the bedroom. In the dark, they changed into their nightgowns and wasted no time getting into bed. She got as close to him as she possibly could. He wrapped his arms around her, feeling her warm body next to his, and then he said, "Good night darling."

"Good night," she replied.

It was somewhere after midnight and pitch black, when the tiny figure slipped out of bed, and started crawling toward the Christmas tree in the next room. She was almost there when she bumped into what she thought was a big grizzly bear. She screamed as loud as she could, and started pounding the big creature with her fist. Bill let out a yell, and everything went silent. For a moment, you could hear a pin drop.

"Ollie, is that you?" asked Bill, taking her by the hand.

"Yes! Thank God it's you," she replied. "What are you doing on the floor?"

"I could ask you the same thing," he said.

They both sat up and stared at each other through the glimmering light from the fireplace. When they realized what each other was doing on the floor, they burst out laughing. Bill made his way to the table where the lamp was. Fumbling around, searching for the matches, he finally found them and lit the lamp. They were still holding their gifts in their hands.

"It's Christmas. Merry Christmas honey," he said, as he handed the gift to her wrapped in brown paper.

"Merry Christmas to you too," she said, as she handed Bill his gift still wrapped in the cloth.

They moved close to the fire and sat down on the floor facing each other. They opened their gifts, Bill waited for Ollie to go first. She took her time un-wrapping the gift. She was so pleased to see the heart locket with the gold necklace. She handed it to him, so he could put it around her neck. She held the heart in her hand, reached over, and kissed him saying, "I love you dear."

"I love you too," he replied, opening his gift. As he opened it, he could hear the sound of the watch ticking in the silence of the night. He was well pleased. He had never owned a watch. He stood up and picked Ollie up, kissed her with a long warm kiss, saying, "I love you, and Merry Christmas. Let's go back to bed."

Chapter Fourteen

Dawsonville was a sight to see. Christmas decorations were still hanging in the windows of all the stores in town. The men had put up extra lamps to make sure everyone could see where they were going. They put the dance platform back down in the center of town. Everyone wanted to make this New Year's celebration the best ever. They had filled many large cans up and down the street with lamp oil and had them burning, so everyone could have a good time and stay as warm as possible. As the custom was, the livery stable furnished a large hog to be bar-be-cued each year. Henry Beckett, the blacksmith, always did the cooking.

People, all the way from Atlanta, came to eat some of his bar-be-cue. Every family brought a covered dish of food and a dessert. They erected a long table just left of where the hog was being cooked. All who brought food placed it on that table. Of course, there was the Elrods and the Longs with their musical instruments, just waiting for the festivities to get started. The word was out that the musicians from Atlanta, those who came to the harvest celebration, would be back to play again.

Ollie and Bill made sure all the chores were finished a little earlier than usual. The cow wasn't all that happy about being milked so early. She kept pawing the ground while Bill milked her. They wanted to be in town by the time the bar-be-cue was ready to eat. The dance would start right after the meal. The snow was still hanging around in some areas, especially in the places where the sun couldn't shine on it very much. Like everyone else, Bill made his way around to the back of the store with the mule and wagon, tying the mule to the hitching rail as soon as they got there. He lifted Ollie down from the wagon and they proceeded to the front of the store.

"Hey you two, we've been looking for you," said Jules, as he came across the street, with Sally holding onto his arm.

"Where did all these folks come from?" asked Bill, shaking hands with Jules, while Ollie hugged Sally.

"I don't know. I guess there are two, maybe three hundred folks here. Some I remember seeing at the harvest celebration. I think some are from Atlanta," said Jules.

"You sure look pretty," Sally said to Ollie. "Is that a new dress you're wearing?"

"Well yes and no. I've never worn it before. Ma made it for me just before our wedding. I wanted to save it for this special night. Ma added some red lace around the hem and the neck to give it a more store bought look. Bill gave me this locket for Christmas." She pulled it out from under the neck of her dress to show Sally.

"It's beautiful," said Sally. "Did you make it to any of your parent's homes during Christmas?"

"We wanted to, but there were so much to do we just couldn't find the time to go."

"We missed you," said Jules. "It wasn't the same without you. Pa wondered all day if you all were going to be able to come. He's really been busy doing something out in the shed behind the barn. It's off limits to everyone. I think Ma knows, but she isn't saying."

Ollie had baked a large pan of her syrup cookies and wanted to set them down on the table. "Let's go to the table and get rid of these cookies then we can socialize a little."

"Let's go. You two want to hang out with us awhile?" Bill asked, Jules and Sally.

"It's good with us," replied Jules. "Sally has been waiting for quite a while for yaw to get here. We came early so we could spend some time with our friends. We also wanted to eat before they started the dance."

"Well let me see what time it is, we don't want to be late for either one," Bill said as he pulled out his watch to check the time. He couldn't resist showing off his new watch.

"Wow, that's something else," said Jules.

Ollie was proud of Bill showing off his watch. Since it was their first Christmas together, she wanted it to be very special. Jules took Sally by the hand and said, "You ready to dance the stars away?"

"I can't wait," she replied, winking at Ollie.

You could hear the music coming from the dance floor area. The men were trying out their instruments making sure they were in tune. Sure enough, the musicians from Atlanta were back with their instruments and tuning up with Eddie and Harris. It sounded very good. When they got close to the dance area, they overheard someone speaking and saying that sometime during the evening, the people from Atlanta wanted to show everyone a new dance. The dancers down there were making it very popular.

―――――✦―――――

By the time the hog was ready to eat, just about everyone in and around Dawsonville had arrived. They were enjoying each other's company, talking and laughing about the good times and the bad. They were discussing things that had happened in their lives throughout the previous year. Some had brought several kegs of home-brew and sat them at the far end of the table. No one was sure, but some thought, the content of one of the kegs, was a lot stronger than the other one. There were plenty to eat and drink. The women had brought several gallons of homemade tea along with their homemade apple cider.

The bell rang at the little court house, everyone knew it was time to gather around the table for their New Year's meal together. The table was filled with dishes of different kinds of food and so many desserts. Everyone had brought something to share. Pastor Robert Moseley led the crowd in an Old Year out and a New Year in prayer. As soon as he said "Amen," everyone lined up and started fixing their plates.

The musicians were already playing their music. You could hear the sound of it from one end of town to the other. The young couples from Atlanta, were already dancing on the old wooden platforms. They were demonstrating the new style of clogging. Paul Crow's two sons, Ron and Lewis, were trying their best to learn the new dance. They had lost interest in learning new things and trying out new ways of doing things. Ever since their mother, Louise, died, they just didn't have the desire to learn or try any new thing. She was the one who wanted her children to learn and know about new ideals. Paul, their Pa, his only thoughts about them learning new things, was he wanted it to be new ways concerning methods of farming and how to make it more productive. Inez, the older sister, had taken it on herself, to follow up as much as she could with her mother's wishes. She was on the dance floor trying to help her brothers learn the new steps.

"Here, let me show you," said Ben, Eddie Long's son. Ben went with his father everywhere. To all the different places his father went to play music. Ever since he was small, and being an only child, he tagged along with his father. His mother died, when he was two years old, with pneumonia. Ben wasn't bashful; wherever his dad played, he was always trying to learn the new dance steps. He wore his red-checkered shirt, with his jeans, and a straw hat, to just about every dance around. It was his style. Ben put his two feet together and let his legs be limber. He raised his feet and legs up and down, and pounded the floor with his shoes, keeping time with the music. Before Inez knew it, she was dancing with Ben.

Ron and Lewis stopped trying to clog and stepped aside. They, along with everyone else, stood on the outside of the dance floor to watch Inez and Ben dance the new style of clogging. With the new dance, you didn't stand single; tapping your shoes on the floor and keeping time with the music, but you held hands with your partner and faced each other while keeping your feet on the floor. The man is to swing the woman around and around landing her back on her feet, while still keeping time with the music. Ben had watched the couples from Atlanta dance for a while, before he tried to do it.

"Let's try it," said Ollie, pulling Bill toward the dance floor.

"I don't know if I can, I always seem to have two left feet when it comes to dancing. But if you are willing I will try with you."

Everyone was having a wonderful time. The new way of clogging gave everyone a desire to learn it. The young couples from Atlanta, quit dancing with each other, and went out into the crowd to get new partners. Ron Crow decided to try again to learn the new dance. He went over and invited Liza Elrod to dance with him. At one end of the platform was Ed and Martha, they wasn't dancing the new steps, but he was swinging her in and out in step with the music, and they were enjoying every minute of it. It was almost midnight and it seemed just about everyone had been on the dance floor, and most had tried the new dance steps.

The courthouse bell started ringing; people who brought their firearms were shooting them into the sky, and everyone gave shouts of joy that filled the air, as the bell rang out the Old Year and rung in the New Year. Everyone stopped what they were doing and gave their partner a Happy New Year's kiss. People were hugging, shaking hands, and wishing each other a very blessed New Year.

"This is the happiest New year I have ever celebrated," said Bill, holding Ollie high in the air. As he slowly let her down, he wished her the best year ever to come her way. Holding her tight, he kissed her with a very long kiss.

"I love you so much," Ollie replied. "I wish this night would never end."

———✦———

A few months have now passed, and Ollie and Bill have settled in, as if they had been together forever. Their love for each other was growing deeper. The old farmhouse had begun to look like a livable place. Ollie still had her flowers, around the old farmhouse and the barn, covered with the pine straw. They had covered them before the bitter cold had set in. She had cuttings from her mother's flowerbeds, sitting in pots inside the house, along with different cuttings of flowers from their friends. She was waiting for warmer weather to put them outside.

Her little runt pig was stretching out real fine. It was growing so fast that Bill was amazed. He marveled at the way she had love and patience for the small animals. Even the small bantam hens never missed a day laying their eggs. Hershel was now a large raccoon. Bill had taken his little house out and replaced it with an opened box where he could hop in and out easily. Ollie was a gentle person and showed the animals love, just as her family and friends had shown her.

Bill was a hard worker. He was up, had the cow milked, the mules and chickens fed, and was waiting for Ollie to finish breakfast. He did all of that before the sun came up. He always left the feeding of the pig to her. He plowed and fixed an acre of land for planting their early crop. They had work hard for the past two days planting the eyes of the Irish potatoes and English peas.

"Ollie, honey, we're getting low on several food items, and this is the week that I'm to meet with the banker in Dawsonville. What do you say we go tomorrow? It would do us good to make the trip." He put his arms around her and gently kissed her and said, "Ollie, I love you so. I don't want to go anywhere without you."

"I know, I don't like to be away from you either. But it's an all-day trip going to town and back, and I'm not feeling too well today." She sat down at the table folding her hands in her lap.

"What's wrong? You're not coming down with something are you?" he asked.

"No honey. It will pass. It just comes and goes. I'll be alright. You go ahead; I'll stay here and take care of things. I'll be alright."

"Okay. I'll leave after breakfast in the morning, and if you don't mind, fix me some of your hoecake to take with me." He took her in his arms and held her tightly. "I'm going to miss you. Are you sure you are all right?"

With a warm kiss, she reassured him she would be all right.

"Ollie, do you think you could milk the cow tomorrow? The old girl seems to have settled down now. It would give me a head start to town if you could."

"I'm scared to death of that cow, there's just something about her that scares me," she replied.

"Are you sure you're not just upset, because I didn't buy that small White-face Hereford you wanted?"

"Of course not," she replied, "I'm scared, but I don't know why. But, if it will help you get home earlier, I'll do my best to milk her."

"Thank you honey, before I leave in the morning I'll tie the cow's head close to the trough. After you get through milking her, you can stand in the hall of the barn and untie her. When you untie her just open the stall door and step out of the way, she will go out to the pasture."

"Well OK, but only because it will let you leave early so you can be back home before dark."

Bill stayed busy throughout the day, cutting fire wood and working on a lean-to, to the barn. He wanted more room to store the feed. By nightfall, he and Ollie were ready for bed. This night seemed to be a special night for both of them. They realized tomorrow would be the first time they have been a part since their wedding.

"Ollie you're the dearest thing to me. I love you so much. Life without you would be my end."

"I love you too," she replied, "just hurry home," wrapping her small arms around him. She didn't sleep much during the night. She kept seeing the cow tied up in the stall, hearing her blow air through her nose, making it sound like a tornado was coming. She dreaded to have to milk her, come morning.

———◆◆◆———

Bill was up, had a warm fire going in the fireplace. The morning was so cold, you were tempted to stay as close to the fireplace as possible. He had fed and watered the mules, tied the cow's head close to the trough like he said he would, and was waiting for Ollie to pack him his lunch. After breakfast, he hitched up the mules to the wagon. She went out on the porch to see him off. He kissed her, holding her close to him.

"I love you honey, I'll be back just as soon as I can. You do be careful," he said as he turned the collar of her coat up to keep the cold wind from going down her neck.

Ollie stood on the porch, with tears in her eyes, watching him and the wagon go out of sight. For the first time in her life she was alone and scared. It felt different. She didn't move from the porch to go inside till she couldn't see him any longer. Shivering, she finally went inside. She stood by the fire for a while. Hershel came out of his warm box, next to the stove, and laid his warm body across her feet. It was as though he was trying to help her get warm. With all the work they had been doing, she hadn't had time to pay very much attention to him. She knelt down, picked him up, and rubbed his warm fur with her hands. "You've been missing me?" she asked.

The raccoon buried his nose inside Ollie's coat and got real still. She continued to rub his fur and talk to him. "I've got things to do Hershel, you just go back to bed for a while and I will take some time with you later," then she put him back in his box. She felt comfortable with the raccoon in the house, having someone to talk to, even though he was an animal, she felt he understood her every word. Now that he was back in bed, it was time for her to get busy. She took the slop to the hog and threw out some grain to the chickens. She knew now the next thing to do was milk the cow. This job, she dreaded more than anything she had ever done. However, she knew it was something that she had to do. She was very slow to pick up the milk pail. Pouring warm water from the kettle on the stove, into the pail, she tightens up the coat around her and heads for the barn. She walked slowly, as she held on to the pail, and even slower as she got close to the barn. She knew in her heart the cow must be milked. She was scared to death to haft to do it. She wanted so much not to show her fear, but her trembling hands gave her away. Some of the trembling was from the cold, but most of it was from fear. She finally reached the barn.

The cow was jerking her head up and down and from side to side making every effort to break loose from the rope. She was pawing the ground with her front hoofs and kicking at the side of the barn with her back ones. She had pawed the dirt floor so much with her front hoofs that she had dug out a large hole in the stall. Ollie set down the milk pail and opened the door of the crib. She took out enough feed for the cow. She took the feed and stood in the hall of the barn, poured the feed into the trough, from outside of the stall. The cow began to settle down as she started eating.

Nervous and trembling all over, she entered the stall with her pail of water and small stool. She sat down on the stool and began to wash the cow's sack. She started humming a few lines from an old hymn. The cow stood still eating her feed, while Ollie finished washing her sack. She remembered once when she went with her Ma to milk, how her Ma would sing to the cow until she was through milking.

Slowly, Ollie began to pull on the cow's teats and milk began to pour into the pail. She paused long enough to unbutton her coat to be more comfortable while she finished milking the cow. She was beginning to feel a little calmer as she continued the milking. She was more than half through, when the cow suddenly started jerking her head and kicking at her with her back legs. Now she was becoming furious. Ollie fell backwards off the stool and spilled the milk all over her and the ground. The cow had managed to pull at the rope enough until she had some slack in it. As Ollie was trying to get to her feet, the cow made a greater effort to jerk some more slack in the rope. When she realized it had happened, she made one final attempt to break it. Jerking her head down with fury, she managed to break the rope. Then she realized, she was no longer tied to the side of the stall. Quickly, the cow turned and got between Ollie and the door. She backed herself as far back as she could with her head down almost touching the ground. Every time she snorted from her nose, the dust would rise from the floor of the stall. Never lifting her head up, she kept pawing the ground. Scared, trembling, and freezing from the milk that had spilled all over her; Ollie started screaming. She knew there was no one to hear her screams, but she kept screaming just the same. She wanted to reach the door and get out. She kept edging herself towards the back wall, trying to get the cow away from the door.

The cow began to paw the ground faster with her hoofs and continued to snort through her nose like a raging bull. She watched every move

Ollie made. Trembling and crying hysterically, she stood frozen with fear, facing the cow with her back against the wall. The cow moved ever so slowly until she was directly in front of her. The cow charged across the stall with her head raised just enough to ram Ollie in the chest pinning her against the wall. She felt the impact break her small bones, as if they were matchsticks. As she was falling towards the ground, the cow made a second lunge, this time striking her in her stomach and slamming her back against the wall. She fell to the ground with blood pouring from her nose, mouth and ears. She lay unconscious, motionless, not moving at all. The cow sensing she had won the victory, moved slowly away from the tiny crushed body, lying on the dirt floor.

Several hours passed, before Ollie regained consciousness. She could hear the snorting of the cow and could feel the pounding of her hoofs on the ground throughout her body. Not knowing just how bad, she was hurt, she tried slowly to move herself. The blood was still coming from her mouth and ears, and now from her eyes.

"Oh my Lord, my Lord," she cried in a whisper, "please help me." She couldn't move herself; her body was in so much pain, that she couldn't think straight. She kept going in and out of consciousness.

Chapter Fifteen

Bill reached Dawsonville around noon. Mr. Dayton, president of the bank, was waiting for him. They had agreed to meet on this date, when Bill bought the farm a year ago. He was looking out through the window of the bank, and he saw Bill, as he was tying his mules to the rail. He came out of the bank and spoke to him.

"Hi Bill. How was the trip? I was hoping to see the little woman with you today. I see you're wearing the new coat you won during the three-legged race."

"Yes sir. It's a mighty fine coat. It keeps a fellow warm with weather like today. The trip coming to town was just fine, no trouble. Ollie wasn't feeling up to the ride today and wanted to stay home and take care of everything. You know Mr. Dayton; this is the first time we have been apart since we were married five months ago."

"Do tell. You and that little lady shore do make a mighty fine couple," replied Mr. Dayton as he patted Bill on the back.

"Thank you sir, I'll be sure to tell her what you said. She will be so pleased."

"Bill, we can do our business before, or after, you've had your dinner."

"If it's all the same to you sir, let's do our business now. Since Ollie is not feeling too good and this is the first time for her to be by herself, I would like to get back before dark."

"Well, come on in the bank son and sit down, we'll get right to the matter." Mr. Dayton took his seat behind his desk and unbuttoned his coat where he would feel more comfortable. He took out his old briar pipe from his desk drawer, packed it with tobacco, lit it up, and said, "There's nothing better than a good smoke while you're doing business. Would you care for one? I have some tobacco paper you can roll you one."

"No thank you. But thanks anyway." Bill set down in the straight chair in front of him. The desk was so large that both parties would have to stand up and lean over it, to shake hands with one another.

"We're right on schedule with our plowing and planting, it looks like we've got a good stand of potatoes coming up. The English peas are almost a foot high now. It took a lot of hard work for us to get the farm ready for spring planting; the place sure was run down."

"I know Bill," replied Mr. Dayton, wiping off some dust that had found its way to his desk. "It's been three years since anyone has tilled that land. The last farmer, who lived on the farm, drank most of the time. He did very little work around the place, some folks seemed to think he might have made moonshine, rather than work the farm. I could have sold the farm several times, if it hadn't needed so much work to get the land ready for farming. Bill, it looks like you and Ollie got off to a real good start. What else can I do for you?"

Bill, crossing his legs, set back in the chair, still a little nervous about doing banking business, he said, "Maybe a few more dollars for cotton and corn seed for planting. We need a few more rations, and I want to buy Ollie a new pair of shoes while I'm in town."

"Son, you don't need money from me for that," replied Mr. Dayton. "Just go over to the General store and have them put what you need on your farm account. We'll settle up at the end of the year. I'm sorry if I didn't make that part clear to you, about how your credit works at the store."

Bill, with a big smiled, uncrossed his legs and stood up. "Well Sir, if you are happy about our agreement, then I'll be going."

"I'm well pleased with you and the little lady having the farm. Next time, you tell her, I insist for her to come to town with you, so we can see her," standing up, he reached over and shook hands with Bill.

He left the bank and crossed the street to the General store, kicking up his heels as he went along. He really felt good. He purchased the seeds and rations they needed, picked out a pair of high snap lace shoes for Ollie, and a sack of peppermint stick candy.

"Bill, I just got in an order of new bed frames. They came with a straw-tick cover," said Charlie, the storeowner.

"What do you mean a straw-tick cover?" asked Bill.

"The bed comes with slats and the cover. The cover was made so you can stuff it full of straw, and it makes a mattress. When the straw gets worn down, you just empty it out, and replace it with new straw," replied Charlie.

"I was gonna buy some more lumber and rope to make another bed. We only have the one I made. How much is the bed frame and cover or straw-tick, as you call it?"

"I will let you have two of them for the price of the lumber and the rope you were going to buy," said Charlie.

"I'll take them. Ollie will be pleased to have something better to sleep on than the quilts we have now for a mattress."

"Bring your wagon around to the back of the store and we can load them there."

"But wait a minute Charlie, I never asked you if I could have them on the credit. I know my farm supplies are good by the bank, but I'm not sure about the bed items. I can't pay anything now; I will pay you when our crop comes in."

"Don't you worry about a thing, the bank will pay me; all you have to do is pay back the bank, they'll see to that."

"Good. Let me take care of my mules and I will come around to the back of the store." Bill went outside, unhitched the mules, and led them over to the watering trough for a drink. After the mules drank their fill, he hitched them back to the wagon, climbed up on the wagon seat and went around to the back of the store. Charlie was waiting on him when he got there. They loaded the seed, rations, bed frames, slats and the covers. He thanked Charlie and climbed aboard the wagon. Taking hold of the lines he said, "Giddy up, it's time to go home."

❦

Several hours had passed; Ollie was becoming conscious enough to open her eyes. Everything was blurred. As she begins to see a little more around her, she tries to move herself very slowly. She could not move without making a groaning sound, the excruciating pain was almost more than she could bear. When she tried to move, she could feel the broken bones in her chest shifting about. As she tried to move, even a small stir, the cow would move also, pawing at the ground with her front hoofs. She was still scared to death. She almost lost consciousness again. She knew if she made a sound or a sudden move, the cow would attack her again. Inside the stall, everything looked so dark to her with all the blood in her eyes. She had to feel her way around on the floor with her fingers, as she desperately dragged her frail broken body, inch by inch toward the door. She could hardly breathe. She knew something bad had happened to her lungs. The deeper she tried to breathe the more excruciating the pain was.

Slowly she worked herself around on the floor, pushing herself with her heels, trying hard to get near the door. With each push, the pain was so severe she would almost pass out. Ollie didn't know just how badly she was hurt, but she felt like she was going to die.

"Oh God," Ollie whispered, "if only Bill were here. Oh Bill, I love you. Please God, help me, please help me."

The cow was now butting her head against the wall. She had won the victory, and wanted out of the stall to celebrate. Every—once in a while she would nudge Ollie's body with her head, making sure her opponent was down, and stayed down. Each time she nudged her, it would send severe pain throughout her body. She passed out twice from the nudging, from all the pain, and the great fear she had of the cow. Each time she woke up, she didn't know just how long she had been unconscious. To her it seemed as if she had been lying there, on the dirt floor of the stall, forever. Somehow, nearly out of her mind with fear and pain she had managed to crawl to the door. Not being able to see clearly she reached out her arm very, very, slowly, and touched the door. She felt the bottom of it and made up her mind to pull herself up and unlatch it.

"I've got to open the door. I've just got to," she kept telling herself. As she managed to lift herself up, she could feel her bones moving and shifting inside her chest. Each time she moved it felt like someone was sticking a knife in her. With blood slowly dripping from her eyes, she prayed, "Lord help me find the latch to the door, please God." There was so much blood coming from her eyes, it made it almost impossible for her to see anything. Her tiny body was racked with pain, but she kept thinking how she could open the door. She couldn't raise herself any higher off the floor. After what seemed like days had passed, she managed to turn enough to face the door. The cow had moved to the back of the stall, still snorting and pawing the ground. She was kicking the pail and stool around in the stall causing them to hit Ollie every now and then. Each time the small body moved, the cow would start snorting again.

It was like a miracle, Ollie stretched up her arm toward the door and with her trembling, cold, stiff, fingers she touched the latch. It was all she could do to try to move it, but it would not move.

"Oh Lord, dear Lord, please help me. I need your strength. I can't do this by myself," she slumped back to the floor, passing out again.

———— ❦ ————

The one thing Bill didn't need to happen was happening. One of the wagon wheels was squeaking very loudly by the time he got near the church. He pulled the reins on the mules heading them in the direction of the churchyard. After stopping, he climbed down from the wagon and unhitched the mules. He gave them a drink of water and tied them to the hitching post at the side of the church. They could rest there, while he worked on the wheel. Bill wanted to fix it as soon as possible, knowing his Ollie was home alone. It was getting late. The more he thought about her, the more he wished he had insisted for her to come with him. He could tell by the squeaking sound, which wheel the noise was coming from. He tried to unscrew the hub, but the weight of the wagon held it tight. The only way he was going to be able to get the hub loose to grease the wheel was to jack up the axle, taking the weight off the wheel. After a few minutes of thinking about how he was going to do this, a thought came to his mind. He would use the hitching rail, the one they tie the animals to on church Sunday. The hitching rail was a long log supported by two posts in the ground. He went to the wagon to get his sledgehammer. Almost every farmer carried the tools he would need for just such an emergency like this in his wagon.

After he got his big sledgehammer from the wagon, he used it to loosen the hitching rail from the two posts. The wooden spikes came loose after a few licks with the hammer. He carried the rail over to the wagon and pushed it up under the axle. Now there was the problem of how he was going to lift the wagon up to free the wheel. He placed a large rock under the rail close to the axle; he then went to the end of the rail and pushed down. The wagon rose from the ground with the greatest of ease, but when he let go of the rail, the wagon would come back down to the ground. Bill couldn't be in two places at the same time. 'How am I going to be able to do this,' he thought. He had to think of something quickly, time was going by fast. He knew he had to hurry up and get home. It was already going to be late for him to get home, without this happening. He went to the well for a drink, and then it happened. Why hadn't he thought of it before now?

He would use the water bucket to raise the wagon off the ground. Bill took the bucket loose from the well, and tied the bucket with some rope; he had in the wagon, to the end of the rail. He started filling the bucket with the heaviest rocks he could find. After putting the heavy rocks in the bucket, the wagon slowly came off the ground. He wasted no time in pulling off the hub. He quickly packed the axle with grease and screwed the hub back on.

Bill emptied the bucket of rocks and untied it, throwing the rope back into the wagon. He took the bucket back to the well and retied it to the rope. He took the rail back to the side of the church and laid it down next to the post. It would have to lay there till he could return to fix it. He didn't have any wooden spikes with him to mount the rail back to the post. He hitched the mules back to the wagon, climbed aboard and headed for home.

━━◆━━

There was no way to tell how long Ollie had been unconscious. After a while, she came to. She was still bleeding from her eyes and nose. With every muscle and fiber in her body, she tried once again to find the latch on the door. This time, after finding the latch, feeling for it with her fingers, she tried to lift it up to unlock the door. Her fingers seemed to have more strength this time. She strained ever muscle in her body trying to lift the latch. After many attempts to move it, the latch moved a little. She pushed it up as slow as she could trying not to bring any attention to her, so the cow wouldn't notice. She was able to move it up little by little. The latch would move up, but when Ollie would lose the pressure with her fingers, it would fall back down again.

The cow kept swishing her tail back and forth hitting the side of the walls. To Ollie, what she was hearing because of all the blood that was in her ears, the swishing of the tail sounded like a drum being pounded a way off in the distant.

With complete exhaustion, she tried once more. She knew in her heart, this was her last opportunity. Her coat felt like it weighed a ton on her body, but it was helping to keep her warm in the frigid stall. The spilt milk had frozen on the ground and on her coat. She was having chills, so violently, that it shook her body all over. Blood was still pouring from her ears. She found the latch again with her fingers. This time, she would not let her fingers relax. Pushing up with all the strength she had left, the latch moved up a fraction this time.

Finally, the latch moved all the way up and the door was unlocked. The door began slowly to move forward. Suddenly, as if someone had made a big push, it swung completely open. Ollie's arm fell to the floor. When the cow saw the door was open, she made a lunge for it. With her head still bowed and snorting from her nose, the cow headed out of the stall. Ollie managed to roll over to one side, as the cow made her way out of the stall; this kept the cow from stepping on her. Still bleeding, exhausted, and with excruciating pain, she passed out again.

***

It was getting a little dusky dark when Bill made it to the off road going to their farm. It wasn't long before he could see the farm in the distance. He was getting excited to see Ollie, to tell her all that had happened and show her the new bed he had bought. There was very little smoke coming out of the chimney. As he got close to the house, he was startled to see the cow outside the pasture fence. She was eating the grass on the outside of the fence near the road. He knew that all Ollie had to do after she finished milking was open the door in one end of the hall of the barn and close the door at the other end, and the cow would have to go out to the pasture. His heart began to beat faster. He whipped the mules with the reins making them run as fast as possible. He was yelling and screaming as loud as he could as he approached the house.

"Ollie, Ollie," yelled Bill. "Oh my God, Ollie, where are you. Say you are all right." He jumped from the wagon even before it completely stopped in the yard, letting the mules come to a full stop on their own. He ran through the front door and out the back, his hat flying off his head as he ran around the house, screaming for her as loud as he could. He ran to the barn and then he saw the stall door open. He rushed to the door. Looking inside the dark stall, he saw Ollie lying on the dirt floor, face down in a puddle of blood. He fell to his knees beside her and began to pray, and cry hysterically.

"Oh my God, what have I done, what have I done?" he cried.

He gently rolled her over and almost fainted when he saw his tiny little wife with blood coming from her eyes, ears, nose, and mouth. She was unconscious and barely alive. With her chest crushed as it was, he didn't know whether to move her or not. He had to make a decision, but what. It was getting so dark he could hardly see what to do. He ran back to the house for the lantern. After lighting it, he rushed back to the barn.

He finally decided to pick her up and take her to the house, but how. He looked around in the barn. Then he decided to rip off one of the wide boards from the loft of the barn to have something to carry her on. He tore the board loose and broke it apart. Taking the short part of the board, he very carefully eased it under her. He ran to the wagon and got the rope he had used earlier in repairing the axle. He quickly took the rope and wound it around her and the board, knowing she would be secure when he picked her up. He was very careful, when he stooped over and picked up his Ollie, board and all. He didn't want to cause her any more pain than she was already experiencing. After he stood up, he headed for the house. She never made a sound when he picked her up into his arms.

"Oh Ollie, Ollie, I love you so. Please don't die. Oh God, don't let her die," Bill pleaded, weeping profusely. He made his way from the barn to the house, and had a little bit of a problem getting up on the porch with her in his arms. He paused for a moment to regain his strength, before going on into the house. He gently laid her on the bed, board and all, and began to untie the rope. He removed as much clothing from her as he could, then he saw just had badly she was hurt.

"Oh my Lord," he said, as he looked at her crushed chest. "What am I going to do?" He poured some water into a pan and began washing the blood from her face. As the cold washcloth touched her face, she moved. She screamed so loud, because of the pain, that Bill was terrified.

"Ollie, Ollie, can you hear me?" he asked.

She nodded her head slightly forward in the direction of yes.

"I've got to get help. You're too badly hurt to be moved anywhere. It's about an hour's trip to the Green's farm; but they are closer than anyone else. Ollie darling, I have to leave you here alone for a while. I've got to get help."

She managed to open her eyes a little bit, with a look of love and understanding; she nodded her head in approval, but still not able to see him clearly. She was having one chill after another. He covered her up with several blankets and quilts. He took time to stir up the fire and placed more wood on it. Kissing her, he whispered softly, "I love you, I love you." He lit the lamp, setting it on the table close to her, and said, "It will be way in the night before I can get back, but I'll be back as soon as I can."

He ran from the house, unhitched the mules from the wagon, put one in the pasture, mounted the other one, and headed for the Green's farm.

———◆❖◆———

He knew the mule was tired from the trip to Dawsonville and back, but he had no choice. He ran the mule as fast as it would go. He had to get help as quick as he could. It was toward midnight when Bill arrived in the yard of Mr. Green's farm. Jumping down from the mule, leaving it to roam in the yard, he ran up on the porch, yelling for Mr. Green. He pounded on the door. The dogs started barking and running out from under the house, ready to bite the intruder. As they came on the porch, growling, and baying at Bill, he turned to yell at the dogs, while he continued to pound on the door.

A light appeared in the house. Mrs. Green came to the door, with a long nightgown and nightcap on and asked, "Bill, what on earth is wrong. What's happened? Shut up dogs! Be quiet. Get off the porch." The dogs walked off the porch very slowly, keeping their eyes on Bill.

"Ollie's been hurt, she's hurt real bad," he replied. "I think the cow might have butted her. Oh, God, it's so terrible. She's home alone. I need you to come. We need help."

Mrs. Green ran through the house to the back porch. She yelled for her husband, Carl. He had been sleeping in the barn for the past few nights. He was keeping an eye on the young heifer, which was due to drop a calf at any time. He came running from the barn as fast as he could.

"What's wrong, what's happened?" he asked. He said hello to Bill as he lit the lamp on the table.

"It's Ollie, little Ollie," she replied. "She's been hurt bad. We have to go to her. She needs our help."

"Bill, put your mule in the pasture. I'll hitch up my horses to our wagon, we can make better time going together, than with you riding the mule and following us," said Carl.

It took Bill a few minutes to find the mule. He had wandered off toward the barn. He finally found him, walked him to the pasture, and turned him loose. By the time he got back to the house; Carl had his horses hitched to the wagon. He woke up the rest of his family, giving them all instructions of what to do while he and Edna were gone. Dianne, the only daughter, was the oldest of the three siblings. She was always in charge when the parents were away. Cody, the next oldest, was given the job of sleeping in the barn to be near the young heifer, in case she dropped the calf. He had helped his Pa several times with cows giving birth. He knew what to do. Randy, the youngest of the three, was to take care of the outside chores.

Mrs. Green quickly changed from her nightclothes and put all her first aid remedies in a bag; she kissed the children and told them they could go back to bed. She put on her bonnet and shawl, grabbed Carl's coat, and headed for the wagon. The horses were prancing about. They weren't used to being worked this time of night. Bill helped Edna up in the wagon and took his seat in the back. No one was saying anything to the other, but you could hear them praying and asking God to be with Ollie. They could hear Bill crying and praying all the way back home.

The trip was much faster going back than it was for Bill coming, because his mule was so tired. Carl knew it wasn't good to run the horses at night. The fear of one of the horses stepping in a hole or a deep rut, maybe breaking a leg, didn't enter his mind. His thoughts were on getting there as fast as they could.

Chapter Sixteen

The fire was slowly burning out in the fireplace. Ollie's body was shaking, not only from the pain, but also from being so cold. Hershel had sensed something was wrong with Ollie. He came out of his box and climbed upon her bed. He crawled underneath the covers and lay as close to her side as he could get. He poked his head out from under the covers and never made another move. Ollie could feel the heat from her furry friend, but wasn't able to speak to him. She did manage to lay her hand on him. She could feel his little heartbeat.

Ollie's mind went back to her childhood. She was hearing her Ma singing and her calling to her while she played with her dolls. She remembered how her Ma was right there when she got her finger caught in a crack in the door, and how she would kiss her every time something happened. Then she heard the church congregation singing an old hymn. She either fell unconscious or just went to sleep; Hershel never felt her move again.

Carl had the horses running most of the way. You couldn't see the lather coming from beneath the horse's collar, but you could smell the sweat. As the wagon rolled into the yard, Bill jumped down and ran into the house. The Green's weren't very far behind. Ollie wasn't moving. It was as if she was dead.

"Ollie, Ollie," whispered Bill, bending down close to her head. "Ollie, honey, I've got Mr. and Mrs. Green here."

Ollie, now so weak from losing so much blood, halfway opened her eyes and tried to speak. With a very faint voice she said, "Hi."

"Bill, you build up the fire and heat up some water. Carl, you can help him," said Edna, pulling off her bonnet and shawl.

As the two men got busy, Mrs. Green started removing the cover from Ollie. When she pulled the covers back, she let out a screamed that caused Bill to drop the wood he had in his arms. Edna almost fainted. Bill and Carl came running to Ollie's bed-side to see what had happened. Hershel poked his head out and then stuck it back under the covers. Seeing what had happened, Bill lifted the covers and took Hershel into his arms. He started rubbing his fur and talking to the little raccoon, trying to help him calm down. Any other time everyone would be bursting with laughter about the raccoon being in the bed, but not tonight.

"What in the world is that?" said Edna, not being able to see too good with the lamp light.

"It's Hershel. It's Ollie's pet raccoon. She has had Hershel ever since he was very little. He must have sensed Ollie was hurt. It was his way of keeping her warm," said Bill as he put Hershel back in his box.

"I'm sorry," she said. "He almost gave me a heart attack. I wasn't expecting to see no raccoon."

Bill picked up the wood and proceeded to rebuild the fire. Edna continued to ease back the covers. She needed to see how she could help Ollie. She opened her coat and was horrified at all the blood she saw. When she managed to cut away some of the clothing, she almost fainted again, as she saw her chest pushed almost to her backbone.

"Oh honey, it's bad, very bad," said Mrs. Green, softly to Ollie. "We've got to get the doctor from town out here," she said to Bill and Carl, wiping some of the blood from her hands. "This child has broken ribs and maybe a lot of other bones broken too. I can't tell. They may have damaged other parts of her body, like her heart and her lungs. I just don't know. I have nothing in my bag that can help this child tonight."

"I'll take one of my horses and go to Dawsonville and find the doctor, it will be sometime tomorrow before I get back. I would go by your folks and let them know about Ollie, but it would take an extra hour for me to do that. We will have to let them know later, if it's alright with you Bill. I will have to let the horse rest some along the way, we ran them pretty hard coming here," said Carl.

"Thank you, Mr. Green," said Bill, "I'll let them know later. I really appreciate what you and Mrs. Green are doing for Ollie and me."

"That's all right," replied Carl, "but, how about calling me Carl, and my wife, Edna, we're your neighbors you know."

"Thanks," said Bill. "If only I had taken the time to milk the cow this morning before I left." Putting both hands in his hair and giving it a hard pull, then putting them together twisting them over and over, he said, "Oh God, why didn't I take the time?"

"Bill, you've got to stop talking like that. This is no time to start blaming yourself. Do you think Ollie got the cow milked before this happened to her? If she didn't that cow is in a pretty bad way. Why don't you check on the cow while I unhitch the horses? I'll ride one of them to Dawsonville, and if you don't mind, put the other one in your pasture," said Carl.

"Go on Bill, check on the cow. While you two are out of the house, I will try to bathe Ollie. She needs you now, so don't let her down," said Edna.

Carl kissed Edna bye, went out, and unhitched the horses. He mounted one and headed for Dawsonville. Bill took the other horse and headed for the pasture. It was so dark he could barely see. He knew the cow was out there, somewhere, and if she didn't make a sound, it would take him a while to find her. He kept walking around in the pasture calling for the cow. Nothing, he heard nothing. It was as if she had disappeared. He didn't even hear a sound from his mule. Then he got an idea. He went back to the barn and got the feed bucket. As he walked slowly through the pasture, he beat on the bottom of the bucket with a stick. The sound drifted across the pasture and through the hollows.

Then he stopped beating on the bucket, and stood still, listening for any kind of sound. Nothing, he continued walking and beating on the bucket. He stopped again, listening. This time he heard some movement to his left. He eased himself over in the direction of the sound. There she was, standing with her head down. What he had heard was her pawing the ground with her hoofs. As he came closer, he could see the cow had the rope that was around her neck, tangled in the barbed wire fence. She was caught so tight, that she couldn't move. He put the bucket down and managed to free the rope from the fence. Bill picked up the bucket, holding tightly to the rope, he led her back to the barn.

The cow didn't put up a fight. She was glad someone had come to her rescue. When Bill got her in the barn, he tied her to the wall as he had done many times before. This time, he made sure she was tied more secure. He lit the lantern that hung in the hallway, and examined the cow's sack. He found that he needed to get the milk pail and milk her. Her teats were swollen almost twice the size they should be, so he knew she needed to be milked.

"How's Ollie doing?" he asked, coming back into the house for the milk pail.

"She's in much pain. I'm waiting for the water to heat up so I can bathe her," said Edna.

"I've got to milk the cow. It's evident Ollie never finished milking her before the accident."

"You take care of the cow; I'll take care of Ollie for now."

Bill headed for the barn and Edna for the warm water. She came back to Ollie's bedside with a pan of warm water and her bag. Her medical bag had seen many days of hard use, from delivering babies, to helping out neighbors with other problems such as, pneumonia, measles, mumps, whooping cough, and several cases of the plain old itch. She took everything out of her bag and laid them on the table beside the bed. She had all kinds of herbs and salves, even a half-pint of moonshine whiskey, but nothing she had brought with her could be of any help to Ollie. She finished cutting away all of her clothes from her waist up. Edna was horrified, as she saw all the damage the cow had done to her little body. She bathed her as well as she could, trying not to cause her anymore pain than she was already experiencing. The warm water felt good to Ollie's skin. It was helping her to quit shivering so much. Some of the blood had dried on her face; it had been there since early morning. She was having a hard time washing it off. By the time Bill came back into the house with the milk, she had her bathed. All the blood that was in Ollie's ears was causing a problem; she could barely hear or understand what anyone was saying to her. Bill took the milk, strained it into the milk jug, and sat it outside on the well. When he came back into the house, he asks if there was anything, he could do to help.

"Yes, you can tear some strips from one of her bed sheets, about five or six inches wide," said Edna. "We'll need them to wrap her up with."

Bill did everything Edna said, and in a few minutes, he had several strips torn from the sheet and handed them to her. He took off his coat, took out the small sack of peppermint candy, and laid it on the table.

"I brought Ollie some candy, she always liked peppermint," he broke and began to cry again.

"That's great. Get a glass and pour it about half full of this whiskey," she said handing the bottle to Bill. "Break up several sticks of the peppermint candy and put them in the whiskey. Stir the candy, in the whiskey, till it dissolves."

He stopped crying and did what she asked him to do. After the peppermint finally dissolved, she gave some of the mixture to Ollie. She helped her drink it out of a spoon, and managed to get most of the whiskey down her.

"Bill, I'm going to need your help. You will need to hold Ollie up enough for me to wrap the strips of cloth around her chest."

"Sure, anything you need for me to do, just tell me." He eased her up enough for Edna to start wrapping the strips of cloth around her chest. She was careful not to wrap her to tight. It took quite a while to get it done, as they were trying not to cause her any more pain, than possible. Ollie had either become unconscious from all the pain or passed out from drinking all the whiskey they gave her. Whatever, she never made a sound while they wrapped her with the strips of cloth. The rest of the night Bill sat by the bed, holding her hands, and stroking her hair. He repeatedly said, "I love you Ollie, I love you." They sat up with her the rest of the night; Bill was by her side and Edna was in the rocker.

As the morning sun began pushing the night away, things began to stir. Edna, rising from the rocker, headed for the kitchen to make breakfast. She could hear the little Bantam rooster crowing out in the yard. It was as if he was telling the world it was time for his breakfast. Bill was still setting by the bed holding Ollie's hand. She was resting as well as she could from all the pain she had. She couldn't move without yelling. The only thing Edna had for the pain was the whiskey in the half pint bottle. She took a few more of the peppermint sticks and put them in the rest of the whiskey that was in the bottle. It would take a little while for them to dissolve. Oh, how Bill wished he could take her pain away. He got up, took the milk pail with some warm water in it, and headed to the barn to milk the cow. Still tied to the wall from last night, she was waiting for someone to come and milk her. He poured the feed into the trough and entered into the stall. He began crying again, when he saw all the blood on the floor of the stall.

For a moment, he wished he had his gun with him; he would kill that cow right there and now.

Then he realized the fault was his. Ollie had told him repeatedly how afraid she was of the cow. She wanted the small heifer instead. He wiped the tears from his eyes and proceeded to milk the cow. After milking her, he turned her loose to go into the pasture. She was glad to be free. Being tied all night to the wall of the barn wasn't any fun for her. He came into the house to strain the milk and was so pleased to see Ollie awake.

Edna took the milk pail from him and said, "I'll take care of this. You sit with Ollie."

Bill didn't hesitate. He gave Edna the milk pail and came to Ollie's bedside, taking her hand in his; he tried to comfort her as much as he could.

"Have you fed the pig?" she asked, in a low whisper.

"No. However, I will. You don't worry about a thing. I will take care of everything. You just get better."

"Bill, take the rest of the whiskey and pour it in a glass. You can use a spoon as we did last night to help Ollie drink it. This will help her with the pain. When you get it all down her, you can take care of things outside. I will have breakfast ready in a little while. I'll prepare some soup for her later. I think she will be alright for a while," said Edna.

"Yes Ma'am," he replied. He took the whiskey and very slowly started spoon-feeding Ollie. After getting it all down her, she went back to sleep. Getting up, he headed outside to finish feeding the animals. By the time he returned, Edna had breakfast on the table. Sitting down they held hands and Edna began to pray.

"Dear Lord, we thank you for your many blessings you have bestowed on us. Now Lord, I have another prayer that needs an answer. You see the condition of little Ollie. All the damage to her frail body, Lord, spare her life. Ollie loves you, she has been faithful all her life to serve you; often with delight, she has gone many times to your house to worship you. Spare her now." Amen.

"Amen," replied Bill.

After a few hours, Edna was able to get some warm soup down Ollie. She hadn't eaten anything since yesterday morning. She took her time in swallowing the soup. Each swallow brought pain to her, causing her to yell out very faintly. Even the half glass of whiskey couldn't stop all the pain she was having. Ollie was able to eat almost a cup of the soup and all the effort it took to swallow it left her very weak, so she went back to sleep.

Hershel had gotten out of his box again, so Edna prepared some food for him. She was still a little afraid of him. This was the first tamed raccoon she had ever seen or been this close to. She watched as he washed his little paws in the small pan of water, Ollie kept close to his box. He always washed, before he would touched his food. After Hershel ate, he jumped up on the bed and lay close to Ollie. He couldn't understand what had happened to his friend. He wanted her to rub his fur and talk to him as she always did. All she was able to do now was lay her hand on him. That was enough for Hershel; he closed his eyes and rested next to her.

It was noon, when Bill and Edna thought they heard a racket outside. Sounds, they were hoping and praying, meant that it was a wagon. It was Carl; he had Dr. Sands with him. They had come from Dawsonville in Dr. Sand's buggy. Carl had tied his horse to the back of the buggy so he could ride with the Doctor. Hurrying into the house, Dr. Sands spoke to Edna and Bill, and then went straight to the bed where Ollie was laying. Carl was outside taking care of the horses. He gave them some water and feed. They had pushed the horses hard to get back to help Ollie.

"Carl, can I fix you all something to eat?" asked Edna as he hugged and kissed her.

"Maybe later, right now let's wait and see what the doctor says about Ollie."

After Dr. Sands examined Ollie, he said to Bill, "She is in critical condition, every rib is broken and her sternum bone is pushed deeply toward her back. It's possible there is damage to her lungs and heart. She's breathing very well considering all the damaged done to her. But, there is one good thing, the baby is all right."

"Baby, what baby?" asked Bill, startled at the news.

"You didn't know Ollie was with child?" asked Dr. Sands.

"My Lord no," he said, putting both hands on top of his head and running his fingers through his hair. "I've been so busy plowing and planting seeds in the ground, that I've hardly noticed anything. It's just that here lately, she hasn't been feeling too well. I should have been more concerned about her needs. I can never forgive myself."

"We have two major problems," said Dr. Sands. "One is, she needs to be in a hospital in Atlanta right now. There, they have some good army doctors that served in the war, and probably have seen bodies as broken and torn as Ollie's. She needs major surgery, but there is no way. She can't be moved. Our hospital in Dawsonville has only two rooms, and we've never had a major case such as this. I'm the only doctor there and I'm not trained nor have I had enough experience to do the kind of surgery she needs. Making a trip, in her condition, that far in a wagon would probably kill her. It's a good day's ride from here to Dawsonville, and no way could we move her to Atlanta. The second thing is, she could take pneumonia almost instantly. She is going to need around the clock attention for quite a while. The broken ribs are pressing on her lungs causing her to be short of breath. She needs all the oxygen she can get, it is even more important, now that she is with child. If she were to move suddenly or turn over during the night, any one of the ribs could puncture her lungs, heart or both."

He took out of his bag some salve and some cotton. With some small wooden spatulas, Dr. Sands wound some cotton around one end and dipped it in the salve. He worked very cautiously trying to remove as much of the dried blood from Ollie's ears as he could.

"I'm going to leave some of the spatulas, cotton, and salve with you. If you will, when you give her a bath, do just what I've done. Just be careful and don't go very deep. It will take a while, but all of the blood will come out."

Hearing all the discussion about her, Ollie began to weep. She knew bones were broken in her body, but never realized just how many, until she heard all that Dr. Sands was saying. Wiping the tears from her eyes, she laid still, afraid to move.

"Edna, I assume you did the binding up.," said Dr. Sands.

"Yes, with the help of Bill, it took both of us to do as well as we did."

"Good job. Yaw did, a very good job," replied the doctor. "With all the damage to her body don't bind her very tight. I'll check the bandages again before I leave." He took from his medical bag, some liquid pain medicine, and left a small bottle of pain pills. "Give her a spoon full of the liquid medicine every two hours for her pain, and after you have used up all the liquid medicine, start her on the pills. Have her take two pills in the morning and two at night. You should have enough to last until I can get back here. I'll try to make it back by the end of the week, and then maybe twice a week after that, if everything is all right in Dawsonville.

I'm going to try to touch base with the doctors in Atlanta and see if they know of anything else I can do. Maybe they will have some advice for me. I know they have two new doctors, who came from New York. I heard they brought with them many new ideas in medicine and surgery. Things change every day in the medical field."

Edna prepared dinner for everyone. She cooked some pork meat with some gravy, biscuits, and fried potatoes. She served it up with a bowl of bean soup. After dinner, Dr. Sands checked the bandages around Ollie's chest again. He made a few adjustments, and then took out of his bag two large rolls of bandages and handed them to Edna.

"I'll bring several more rolls with me when I return. She will need a lot more before this is over. If you need to, you can wash these bandages and reuse them." He had done all he could do, and was ready to return to Dawsonville.

"I'll cut over by the Voyles' on my way back to town and tell them about their daughter. I'm sure they will want to know," said Dr. Sands, picking up his bag, and putting on his coat.

Bill followed the Doctor out to his buggy. "Sir, I don't know how to thank you for coming. I can't pay you anything right now, but I will as soon as I can."

"Son don't you worry about my bill. You just take care of the little woman. She's going to need all the help everyone can give her."

Bill helped the Doctor into his buggy and thanked him again. The Doctor touched the reins to his horse and rode out of sight.

Chapter Seventeen

"Carl, if it's alright with you, I'll stay with Ollie and Bill until the Voyles' can be told, and get here. I'm sure they will work out some way to come and help Bill."

"Sure honey. You stay as long as you feel to. I just need to get back to the farm. The little heifer may have dropped her calf by now. The children and I can handle things till you can come home," he replied.

"Thanks for understanding," replied Edna. "When you get home you try to rest some. Let the children help out by doing most of the chores till you do get some rest, OK?"

"I'll get some rest. I promise. Bill, if it's alright, I'll go by the Weldon's and tell them about Ollie? I know their daughter, Sally, loves Ollie. They've been best friends for as long as I can remember. I'm sure they will want to know."

"Sure thing, that would be good of you to do that," he replied. "I'll help you with the horses." Bill went to the pasture, rounded up the horses, and helped Carl hitch them up to the wagon. Carl kissed Edna bye, took time to tell Ollie he would be praying for her and kissed her on her forehead. He shook hands with Bill, climbed up on the wagon, and headed out.

"Edna, I've got to put up the wagon. It's been sitting right where I left it, when I came back from Dawsonville," said Bill, coming back into to the house.

"You go and do what you haft to do. I think Ollie will be alright for now."

In a few minutes, Bill came running back into the house and said, "You know what? I plumb forgot about the two bed frames and straw-tick covers I bought in Dawsonville yesterday." Coming to Ollie's bedside he knelt down and said, "Honey, I bought you a new bed. It came with a straw-tick cover. All we have to do is set it up, put the slats across it, and fill the cover with straw. After we put some quilts on it, you will have a bed to sleep on just like they do in town. I am gonna put one in each room so we can have a fine bed for our company. What do you think about that?"

Ollie smiled. Only her Bill would have thought about buying her a new bed. He got busy and set the beds up, one in each room. He took the covers to the barn and filled them with straw, packing them tight so they would stay puffed up for a few nights at a time. When he brought them back into the house, Edna helped him put them on the beds and fixed the covers, now the beds were ready for anyone to sleep on.

"It will be awhile before Ollie can be moved to the new bed," said Edna. "Right now the bed she is lying on is stiff enough to keep her body straight and her bones from moving."

Bill placed one of the new beds close to the one Ollie was on, and sat up the other one in the other bedroom. He lay down on the new bed. He was close enough to touch her and to hear her if she needed anything. Edna slept on the other new bed. This was good for her; she hadn't stopped since she had gotten there, she was very tired. Bill and Edna got some sleep, while Ollie was in and out of it, all night long.

Carl made his stop at the Weldon's a few hours before dark. He was also trying to get to his farm, if he could, before dark. When he pulled his wagon into their yard, he was pleased with the welcome he received from them. Jack, Ethel, and Sally were standing on the front porch waiting for him. The dogs had heard Carl's wagon coming, and started barking, before they were able to see him. So the Weldon's knew in advance, they were going to have company.

"Good to see you Carl," spoke Jack, stepping down off the porch. "What brings you out this way? Get down and rest yourself. Ethel, get Carl something to drink."

"No, no, no, that's just fine. Don't bother. I've got to be going on home shortly. Thank you any way. I haven't been home for a day or so. I need to get there, before it gets too dark to check on things. I just came by to tell you folks about Ollie."

Everyone's ears perked opened. Ethel sat down in a rocker on the porch and Sally stood behind her holding onto the chair. It was very seldom anyone came just to bring news about some happenings. The last time was ten years ago. Then, it was a rider going through the county telling everyone the new courthouse and jail was ready to serve the public. It had taken them close to a year to get the courthouse finished, so they wanted the community to know it was finished. The Weldon's were anxious to hear what Carl had to say.

He told them all he knew about Ollie and her accident. What the Doctor had said and how Edna was staying for a few days to help them out.

"I can stay with Ollie for a while, can't I Pa? It will be several weeks yet, before there is any planting for us to do," said Sally, stepping down off the porch to stand next to him.

"This kind of accident must be mighty hard on them," said Jack putting his arm around Sally. "We'll see. Much oblige to you for coming this far out of your way to tell us about Ollie."

"You just wait a minute, Carl Green," said Ethel, getting up out of her rocker. "I'm going to pour you some tea in a fruit jar. You can take it with you." She headed into the house. When she came back, she gave him the fruit jar filled with tea, and some biscuits filled with ham. Handing them to Carl, she said, "We'll go to Ollie and Bill's in the morning and check on them, and in the meantime, we'll talk about what we can do tonight," as she looked at Carl and Sally.

"Thanks for the tea and biscuits. I better be going," said Carl. He turned the horses around in the yard and headed home. It was way after dark when the horses finally pulled the wagon into the yard. Carl was glad to be home. Yet his mind was on Ollie and all she was going through. He put the horses in the pasture and came quietly into the house. He managed to crawl into bed without waking the children.

⟞⟨⬦⟩⟝

Dr. Sands was as good as his word. It was late in the evening when he got to the Voyles farm. Ed was pitching down some hay from the loft of the barn for the horses in the corral. He spotted the buggy coming a good ways off. By the time, the buggy pulled into the yard; he had finished pitching the hay down and was waiting to see who their company could be. Ed was very surprised to see it was the doctor.

"What in the world brings you so far from town?" asked Ed, helping the doctor down from his buggy.

"Well, Ed, I've got some bad news. Is the rest of the family here? I would like to talk to all of you together if it's possible."

"Sure, Martha and Jules are in the house. Martha has just about got supper done." Ed walked the horse and buggy over to the rail, and tied the horse to it. Then he walked into the house with Dr. Sands.

"Hello Dr. Sands," said Martha, wiping her hands with a towel. "What are you doing out here? I don't know of anyone having a baby around this time. What's going on?"

Dr. Sands pulled up a chair and sat down. He started telling the family about Ollie, what had happened to her, and the condition she is in now. Then he said, "Not all is bad, I have some exciting news to tell you. Ollie is with child."

"Dear Lord! Oh my God," cried Martha, leaving the stove and joining Dr. Sands at the table. "Why haven't they told us before now?"

Ed moved over to where Martha was sitting and put his arm around her. Jules took a seat at the end of the table. With tears in his eyes, he stayed quiet, heartbroken over the news of his little sister having such a horrible accident.

"No one knew except Ollie. Bill didn't know himself till this happened," replied Dr. Sands. "I found out about it when I examined her. She is about four, maybe five months along, as much as I could tell. I think the baby will be all right, it seems to have a strong heart beat."

"Well, we'll go there the first thing in the morning," said Ed. "Whatever we can do for her we will." He turned his back to the family, hoping they couldn't see the tears rolling down his face. Martha and Jules were crying also. Just the thought of their Ollie being so badly hurt broke their hearts. After a while, she pulled herself together and finished cooking supper.

"It's so late Dr. Sands; would you please have supper with us and spend the night? It would be dangerous for you to travel on the road with it being so dark. We have an extra room and you can start out early in the morning," said Ed.

It didn't take Dr. Sands long to make up his mind. "Sounds pretty good to me," he replied. "I'll take you folks up on it. First, I need to take care of my horse."

"I will do that for you," said Jules. "Keep your seat. I will feed your horse and turn him into the pasture, and I will catch him for you in the morning."

<hr />

Carl awoke the next morning with the sound of pots and pans rattling in the kitchen. He got up, put his overalls and brogans on, and made his way into the kitchen. He spoke, "Hi honey," to Dianne. She jumped; she was so startled to see her Pa home.

"What time did you get in? Is Ma with you?" Dianne asked.

"It was pretty late when I got here. No, your Ma stayed with Ollie. Ollie had a very bad accident. She is in bad shape. Is Cody still sleeping in the barn?"

"Yes. He said last night that the calf would more than likely drop today. Cody was hoping you would be back before it happened. He has prepared everything that he would need to help the heifer deliver her calf, in case you didn't make it back. Sit down Pa; I'll have breakfast in a little bit. Randy is outside feeding the rest of the animals.

"While you are finishing the breakfast, I'll check on Cody and the heifer," said Pa.

When Randy saw his Pa in the yard, he made a dash over to him. He was so pleased to see him. This was the first time both of his parents had been away at the same time. Carl put his arm around him and fluffed his hair with his other hand. Randy didn't mind it this time, because he was so glad to see his Pa.

"Is Ma in the house?" asked Randy, hoping his Pa would say yes.

"I'm sorry son; your Ma had to stay with Ollie. Ollie has been hurt very bad. She will be home in a few days. Until then, you children will haft to do with me."

Randy walked with his Pa to the barn where Cody was still working with the young heifer. She was lying on some straw trying to push the calf out.

"Good morning Pa," said Cody, when he saw Carl come into the stall.

"Good morning son. How's she doing?"

"She's having a pretty rough time of it. She's been up and down, several times during the night. It looks like she could drop any minute."

"Let's see if we can help her in any way," said Carl, taking the position where Cody had been. He pushed the heifer a little bit trying to get her to stand up. After a few tries, she stood up and when she did, the calf's head started poking out. She lay back down and then stood up again. With all her strength, she pushed hard. Right before their eyes the calf was born. It was a little heifer, just like her mother. They started dancing and rejoicing together, and then Randy ran to the house, yelling for Dianne to come and see the new calf. She dropped everything and came running. When she entered the stall, she couldn't help but cry, as she saw the miracle of the birth of the little calf. The mother cow was licking her young calf, as if to say how much she loved her.

At daybreak, Ed and Jules had already fed the horses and were hitching them up to the wagon. Martha had breakfast on the table waiting for them to come inside. Jules would wait and go later in the week to check on Ollie, for now he was going to stay home, and take care of the animals, while his parents were gone.

After breakfast, Jules said, "I'll clean up everything, yaw go ahead. It will do Ollie good to see you."

"Thank you son," said Martha, getting up to put her coat on.

"Just keep your eye on things till we get back," said Ed, hugging Jules.

Ed helped Martha up in the wagon. With a light touch of the reins to Big John, they were on their way. Instead of talking to each other during the trip, they used the time to talk to God about the situation. It was noon, when they got to Ollie and Bill's farm. Bill greeted them as soon as they arrived in the yard. He was so nervous. He didn't know how they were going to accept him, since he was the one that left Ollie at home to milk the cow. He helped Martha down from the wagon. It was hard for him to look at her with tears flowing down his cheeks.

Martha put her arms around Bill hugging him very tight, and said to him in a low gentle voice, "I'm so sorry Bill, that this has happened to our Ollie. I know how much this must hurt you too."

"Thank you Ma'am" he said, as the tears rolled down his cheeks. "I'm so glad you're here."

Ed got down from the wagon; tied Big John and Belle to the hitching rail, and came over and shook hands with him. He could tell Bill was hurting deeply. Without saying another word, they all went inside the house. Martha went straight to Ollie's bedside, kneeling down she kissed her over and over, telling her how much she loved her, as she stroked her hair. Ollie reached up trying to touch her Ma's face. Martha took hold of her hand and rubbed it all over her face, letting Ollie feel her skin. After a few moments, she rose up, and gave way for Ed to kneel down by Ollie. Martha went over to Edna, put her arms around her, and thanked her for being there to help her daughter and Bill.

Ed kissed Ollie's hand and said, "I love you darling. I have been praying for you to get better. I'm so sorry this has happened to you." As he got up from her bedside, now knowing they would be there more than just today, he asked Bill if it would be all right to turn his horses loose in the pasture.

"Sure. I will help you with them. The cow is in the pasture, but I don't think she will hurt your horses. She hasn't tried to hurt my mules."

Leaving Ollie alone to rest, Martha and Edna went into the kitchen to talk and prepare dinner.

"Martha, Ollie is really hurt bad. I know Dr. Sands told you about her, but I want you to know when you give her a bath, not to be shocked at what you will see. Don't let on to her, just how bad it is, at least not right now. She knows that she is hurt, but she doesn't realize how bad it is yet," said Edna.

Setting down at the table, after listening to what Edna had just said, Martha put her hands over her mouth as she began to weep. She didn't want Ollie to hear her weeping. "Lord, I remember the dress I made for her just before she married Bill. How she would try it on and dance around the room making the tail of it swirl way out, she was so happy." Martha couldn't help it. She broke down again crying and saying, "my poor little girl, oh my poor little girl."

"You must stop that. She mustn't ever see you showing her pity. You've got to be strong for her sake. She needs you now more than ever in her life," said Edna, putting more wood in the stove.

Wiping the tears from her eyes, Martha stood up and said, "You're right. I know you're right. I can't fail her now"

After turning the horses into the pasture, Bill and Ed came back into the house. Ed went to the kitchen where the ladies were; Bill went straight to the bed, and sat close to Ollie.

"Ollie, darling, please pull through this. I need you, we all need you, and I love you so. If you didn't know it before, you are with child, and the baby is fine," he said, as he gently rubbed his hands over her stomach.

Ollie smiled and spoke very low to Bill, "I thought maybe I was, but wasn't sure. I was waiting to talk to Ma. I was going to talk to her on Sunday at church about how I was feeling, the way I was getting a little nauseated every once in a while, especially in the mornings. I didn't want you to worry about me with all you've been doing. The pain is so terrible. Oh Bill, I tried to do what you said, but the cow seemed to know I was scared of her. She broke loose, and I had nowhere to go."

"That's all right," said Bill, "I'm so sorry. You just concentrate on getting better. I'll take care of everything. I promise. I'm so sorry."

The next morning found Martha and Edna in the kitchen fixing breakfast. "What did you think about the new bed Bill bought? Did you sleep well on it?" asked Edna.

"It was good; Ed kept turning over and over on it. It will take him some time to get used to it, but we rested well."

Ed was taking care of the livestock while Bill milked the cow. It was a hard thing for him to do, since he knew the cow had hurt his Ollie. Martha and Edna were very close friends. One time, when Edna's daughter, Dianne, almost died with pneumonia, it was Martha, who came with her mother's recipe made of herbs, and wrapped Dianne's chest with it. Then she stayed for a few days to keep a watch on her.

"Martha," said Edna, while she was wiping off the table preparing to set it with the plates and coffee cups, "I think when Bill leaves to go tell his family about Ollie, I will go with him. He can drop me off at my house on his way there. Right now we've done all we know to do. The house is not large enough for us all. What do you think?"

Putting her arms around Edna, she said, "You have done more than enough. The way you took care of Ollie, the doctors couldn't have done better. You're right about the room. Ed and Bill haven't been sleeping very much. They take turns, during the night, keeping the fire going in the fireplace. I know it gets pretty cold during the night and they have tried to keep the house warm."

Ed and Bill got through with the chores and came back into the house. Bill took time to strain the milk and put it out on the back porch, where it was cold. When the women finished cooking breakfast, they placed it on the table, and then they all sat down to eat. Taking hold of each other's hands, Bill began to pray. "Lord Jesus, we give you all the glory today and thank you for your many blessings you have shared with us. Give Ollie the strength to come through this, and give us the courage to stand with her through it all. Amen."

They all ate hardily, and then the women cleaned up the kitchen. Ollie was talking a little stronger. She was able to eat some soft scrambled eggs with a glass of milk for her breakfast.

Bill came over to her bedside, and knelt down, kissing her on her lips, he said, "I've got to let Pa and Ma know about you. They will be hurt if I wait any longer to tell them."

"I know dear. You go do what you have to do, I will be alright," she replied.

"I'll be back sometime this afternoon. I love you," he said as he went out to hitch up the mules.

Coming over to her bedside, Edna spoke very softly, "Ollie, honey, we're praying that you get better soon. I must be getting back home today. You're gonna be just fine now that your folks are here. I'll be back in a few days." She bent down, kissed Ollie on her cheeks, and squeezed her hand. She said her goodbyes to Ed and Martha, put on her coat and bonnet, and picked up her bag and went outside. Bill was waiting on her. He helped her up into the wagon, climbed aboard and spoke to the mules to be moving. Ed stood in the yard and watched them till they drove out of sight. He knew without Mr. and Mrs. Green, his Ollie wouldn't have made it. For the next few days, Ed took over the job of milking the cow and tending to the livestock.

Chapter Eighteen

Carl was surprised to see Bill and Edna coming into the yard. He had just come from the barn, leaving the heifer there as she let the calf nurse for its breakfast. Cody was staying with the heifer while Carl went for more feed.

"Hello darling. Hi Bill, how's Ollie this morning?" asked Carl.

Bill, climbed down out of the wagon and said, "She is resting as well as possible. Her condition is about the same. I'm on my way to tell my folks about her."

"Can you stay for dinner? I think Dianne has it about ready," said Carl, helping Edna down from the wagon.

"Thanks, but no thanks. I best be going. I want to make my trip to Pa's and get back home before it gets too late." He climbed back up in the wagon and said, "Thank you all again for what you have done. I couldn't have made it without you."

"That's alright. We will come back soon," said Edna.

Bill turned the mules and wagon around and headed out. Carl put his arms around Edna and told her to set her bag on the ground. "Before we go in the house, I want to show you the little calf. She shore is pretty," said Carl, as they headed for the barn.

<hr/>

It was mid-afternoon when Bill got to his folks. The sound of the dogs barking brought Tom and Mattie out on the porch. They were pleased to see Bill, but disappointed they didn't see Ollie with him. Tom stepped down off the porch and took hold of the mules' bridles as they came to a stop in the yard.

"So good to see you, son," said Mattie, as Bill stepped down from the wagon. Putting her arms around him, she asked, "What in the world brings you by without little Ollie?"

"That's what I've come to tell you. Ollie is hurt very bad. The cow butted her, while she was trying to milk her day before yesterday," replied Bill.

"Oh my God, have you gotten a doctor for her?" asked Mattie.

"Yes, that's why I haven't come to tell you before now. The Greens were closer than anyone was; they came and helped until this morning. Carl went after the doctor while I stayed with Ollie and Mrs. Green. The doctor went by on his way back to town and told Ollie's folks. They are with her now, so I could come and tell you about her."

Tom turning the bridles loose came over and patted his son on the shoulder. "What can we do to help you?"

"Right now, I just don't know. The doctor will be back this weekend and we all hope he brings us some good news. For now, Ollie can't be moved. She has broken bones all in her chest. She's with child; and the doctor says she is about four or five months along."

"When we were there with you killing the hog, why didn't you tell us about Ollie being pregnant?" asked Mattie.

"Ma, I didn't know myself till day before yesterday," Bill replied.

"I thought you were going to do all the milking," said Tom. "You knew how scared she was of that cow."

"I know. It's my entire fault." He broke down and started crying. He couldn't help it. Every time he thought about the incident and about his Ollie being so hurt, he cried. Sobbing, he said, "I thought the cow was tame enough now so she could milk her. I had to go to town to take care of business, so I asked her to milk the cow. I wanted to leave early, so I could get back before it was too late."

"Come on in and let me fix you something to eat. You must be worn out," said Mattie, patting him on his back.

"No, Ma, but thank you. I must get back to Ollie as fast as I can."

"Tom, if it's alright with you, I will go back with Bill and see what I can do to help? You can come tomorrow after you get through taking care of things here."

"That will be alright," he replied.

Mattie went inside the house to get her things. She was gone quite a long time. When she returned, she had a basket filled with food. She had on her coat and bonnet and was ready to go. Tom helped her up into the wagon. Bill put the basket in the back of the wagon, climbed up, and saying goodbye to his Pa. They left for home.

———◆◈◆———

Ed had rounded up the cow from the pasture. It was time to get the milking done. Martha was fixing supper and talking to Ollie while she worked. The cook stove was nice and hot helping to warm the house and to do the cooking. Before Ed went to milk the cow, he had also built a nice size fire in the fireplace.

Martha had the milk pail waiting for Ed when he came back in. On his way back to the barn, he took with him, a bucket of slop for the hog. After feeding the hog, he threw some grain out for the chickens. They had been faithful every day to lay their eggs.

"Are you feeling any better?" Martha asked Ollie.

"I feel some better. But I can't move without severe pain in my chest."

"I'm sure the pain is terrible. I'm so sorry this has happened to you. Honey, why didn't you tell me about the baby?"

"I was going to Ma. You were going to be the first one for me to talk to. I wasn't sure I was pregnant, but I thought I was. I knew you would know. I didn't want to tell Bill till I was sure about it."

"Well, don't you worry yourself about it. You concentrate on getting better," said Martha.

"We talked about a lot of things before I got married, but we never discussed anything about having babies."

"I know dear. I was going to, but different things kept coming up, and I thought I had plenty of time to talk to you about it later. I'm sorry."

Ed made it okay milking the cow. He did what Bill told him to do. He tied her head to the wall of the stall till he got through milking her. Martha strained the milk and set it outside to keep it cool. By the time she had supper ready; Bill was coming back into the yard with his Ma. He helped her down, then picked up the basket of food, and carried it into the house.

"Hello Martha," Mattie said, as she gave her a hug, then shook hands with Ed. She went to Ollie's bedside. "How are you dear? Bill told us all about what happened." She knelt down, and kissed Ollie on her cheek. "You are the only daughter-in-law I will ever have, and I love you as a daughter. We are going to see you through this. You and the baby are going to make it through this and be o.k." She started rubbing Ollie's arms.

Bill sat the basket of food down on the table, and came over and stood at the foot of Ollie's bed giving her one of his big smiles. She felt better knowing he was back. After supper with things put away, Ed, Martha and Mattie sat around the fireplace talking. Bill sat close to Ollie as they listened to their parents talk about their lives and everyday happenings.

❧

It's Saturday morning, all the livestock has been taken care of, the cow milked, and the chickens fed. They all were looking forward for Dr. Sands to return today; hoping he would bring some good news from Atlanta. They were hoping he had good news, after talking to the other doctors, of some way to help Ollie more.

"Martha," said Ed, "after the doctor comes, and if Ollie is stable, I'll go back home and help Jules with the work. I'm sure he will want to come Sunday to see Ollie."

"That will be all right," she replied.

They all gathered at Ollie's bedside and prayed.

After prayer she said, "My chest is so sore I can hardly move."

"That's all right, if you need to move or turn let me know, I'll help you," Bill replied.

"How bad am I?" she asked.

"We don't really know. You have been hurt real bad. We'll know more when the doctor returns." He really didn't want to tell her just how bad he thought she was.

"Dr. Sands was going to talk to some of the younger doctors in Atlanta. They are experts in the field of broken bones. He is hoping, he can come back to see you with some new medical information" said Martha.

"Now don't you worry," said Ed, "just try to get better."

"But Pa, my chest and back hurts so badly. I can't move. I can hardly breathe. My chest is pushed almost into my back bone, I can feel it there," she said, rubbing her hands across her chest.

Bill quickly made it to the kitchen, before he broke down, crying. He couldn't help it. He felt so guilty about it all. He didn't haft to buy the cow, but he did. He didn't haft to leave her to milk the cow, but he did. All this was in his heart and going through his mind. He felt the pressure of it all so deep inside of him. It was almost impossible for him to bear it.

"Now, now, Bill, be strong. Ollie needs you now. We are all going to help her through this," said Martha, coming into the kitchen putting her arms around him.

———❖———

It was near noon when Dr. Sands did show up. Bill and Ed were busy in the yard cutting up more firewood. When they saw Dr. Sand's buggy coming in the distance, they stopped what they were doing, and waited for him to come into the yard. They greeted the Doctor and were so glad to see him. Ed helped him from his buggy, while Bill held the horse's bridle. As soon as the Doctor's foot hit the ground, Bill had the horse tied to the hitching rail. They all headed into the house. Martha greeted the Doctor with a welcoming handshake. Everyone was anxiously waiting to hear what the doctor had to say. Bill went to the opposite side of the bed and knelt on the floor. He never took his eyes off Ollie.

"How you been doing?" asked the doctor.

"Pretty well," replied Ollie. "I still haven't been able to move. When I breathe a deep breath it hurts me all over."

Dr. Sands pulled back the covers and took a long time listening to her heart and lungs. He felt all around her chest. Finally he said, "Ollie, you are blessed to be alive today. Only God kept you alive through all that happened to you."

Ollie, holding to Bill's hand, asked Dr. Sands, "Will I ever be able to do anything again, like my house work, working in the yard, helping Bill, and feeding my runt pig? Will I be able to walk all right? Will I lose my baby? Can I have more babies? What, What," was the questions Ollie wanted to hear answers to. Tears were flowing, not only from Ollie, but, also, from everyone in the room, including the doctor.

After he finished examining her, he said, "I've got some good news and some bad news. The good news is that your baby is doing very well. Its' heartbeat is normal. The bad news is, after talking to the doctors in Atlanta, they all agreed there was nothing anyone could do for you out here on the farm. You would have to be in Dawsonville and they would come from Atlanta to see you. However, you can't be moved to the hospital in Dawsonville due to the severity of your broken bones and the threat to the baby. Even if it was possible to move you, they are not sure, if they could do anything to help you. I told them everything I knew about you, and what I had seen about your condition. What they suggested was to keep you wrapped as tight as you can stand it and let nature take its course for now. Since you are breathing all right, your lungs must be okay, your heart seems strong. The only thing we can do is wait it out. After the baby is born, we might have a chance to get you to Atlanta, and let the other doctors have a good look at you."

Ollie began to weep again, and so did everyone else. Even Dr. Sands had tears in his eyes again. He had known her all her life. He was the one who helped deliver her sixteen years ago.

"You rest all you can, and when you feel like you could sit up, try. Pneumonia has a way of getting into you, when you have to lie flat, and can't move. You don't need that. You have enough trouble as it is. I'll see you in a few weeks. I wish there were more that I could do for you. Drink a lot; eat as much as can, you need strength for yourself and the baby." He handed Martha the sack of bandages he had brought with him, along with more pills for her pain. The wrappings around her body would not have to be changed as often now. The doctor didn't even remove them for his examination.

Everyone was disappointed at the Doctor's news. However, no one let Ollie know how they felt. They all knew it was going to be a hard road for her for the next few months, or even more. Dr. Sands said, "I must be going. It will be mighty late by the time I get back to Dawsonville." Bidding all a good day, he headed outside to his buggy. Ed followed him out and helped him water his horse. When the doctor was out of sight, he was still standing in the yard thinking about what the Doctor had said about his little girl.

<hr>

It was late in the evening when Dr. Sands got as far as the church, on his way back to Dawsonville. The pastor and several of his members, who lived close to the church, were there working. They were cleaning up the grounds, getting things ready for the big day on Sunday. The Elrods and the Longs were busy repairing the hitching post. The Doctor stopped when he saw the crowd. He wanted to water his horse, and to tell the pastor and the group of men working, what had happened to Ollie and Bill.

"I'll be sure that everyone knows tomorrow about Ollie. We will have a special prayer for her and the family. I know many of the folks will want to help them in every way possible," said Pastor Mosley.

"I see you are repairing the hitching post. Bill told me how he had to repair his wagon wheel here at the church, and how he used the hitching rail to lift the wagon up, so he could grease the axle," said Dr. Sands.

"We were wondering why the rail was lying on the ground, when we got here today. The men are repairing the rail now. Everything else is okay," said the pastor.

"Well I better be getting along, it will be dark before I get back to Dawsonville."

"Thanks for stopping by to let us know. We all are very fond of those children," said the pastor.

People came from different parts of the county. The churchyard was filling up with wagons and buggies, and the church was filling up with people. Pastor Mosley was taking his time to greet everyone as they came through the door. The second row on the right side was empty. The Voyles weren't there yet, neither were the Franklin's, they usually sat on the left side. The people of the congregation were whispering among themselves, where could these families be, it was not like them to miss church.

The sound of the organ playing was a summons to everyone to come inside the church. The choir led out with, "What a Friend We Have in Jesus," and Katie McClure was encouraging everyone to join in and sing. When the singing was over, the pastor took the pulpit and started with a prayer. As he began to speak, he wiped the perspiration from his forehead, even though it was still cold weather. After a few attempts at trying to clear his throat, he began to talk and say, "Brothers and Sisters, we have a serious prayer request. You all know little Ollie Voyles, who is now married to Bill Franklin, well; she has had a horrible accident. It seems their cow butted little Ollie in the chest, driving her into the wall of the stable, as she tried to milk it. She is critical and needs our prayers and our help. Church let us pray."

The whole church joined in the prayer, with many weeping, as they held each other's hand. Pastor Mosley's sermon was about, "When you see your brother in need." The whole congregation received his message with thoughts of Ollie and Bill's needs.

When the church service was over everyone went outside to spread his or her dinner. After dinner, the people spent the afternoon talking about Ollie, and how each one could help. Jack Weldon spoke up and said, "My family and I are going this evening to visit with them, if there's anything you folks want to send, I would be more than pleased to carry it to them."

Lot of the food, which the folks had brought for their dinner, found its way into a basket, that someone had set out just for Bill and Ollie. When the dinner was finished, the Weldon's loaded up their wagon to head out. Several of the people sent words of encouragement to Ollie and Bill, and the farmers told Jack, to tell Bill, not to worry about getting his crop in the ground. That the men in the community were getting together to work out a plan to help him. They weren't very far out of sight of the church folks, when Sally began pleading with her Pa to let her stay and help Ollie.

"You know she would do the same for me. Even her folks would let her do it. Please Pa, let me help them."

"You know, you're the only help your Ma has, when I'm in the field or gone somewhere," replied Jack.

"Don't you worry about me any, I can handle whatever needs be done till she gets back," replied Ethel.

"Well alright, you can go and stay awhile, but we'll have to go by home, and get you some extra clothes," said her Pa.

"Oh thank you Pa," she said, stretching forward enough to give him a hug around his neck.

When they got near Little River, Jack stopped the mules. He stood up in the wagon and pointed down the river. He spoke softly to Ethel and Sally, saying, "There's a strip of bottom land, about ten acres down that way, the bank wants to lease or sell the land. It is some prime land for raising corn. I've been thinking about putting in more corn. The market was good last year and we could shore use the money. What do yaw think about it?"

"Do you think we can handle more land now? Seems we got our cup full as it is," replied Ethel.

Sally was being very quiet about it all. She knew if Jules Voyles would ever ask her to marry him, she would say yes before the clock could strike another minute.

"I can handle the ten acres by myself, if need be. Corn is half the trouble that cotton is. Just something for all of us to be thinking about," said Jack, as he started up the mules again.

Sally was relieved that her Pa said he could handle the extra acres by himself. She knew if Jules would ask her to marry him she would. She had waited for him ever since they were children. The wagon made its way on down the road with no one saying a word, each one with their thoughts going in different directions. Sally was daydreaming about her life, what it would be like to be Mrs. Sally Voyles. Jack had visions of long rows of corn, Ethel, looking at Sally, was thinking that one day soon, her baby would be facing the world without her. She could see it coming, every time she saw the look on Sally's face, when she was around that Voyles boy.

By the time the wagon came to a full stop, Sally was already in the house putting some of her clothes together. Ethel followed her to her room. This was the first time her little girl was going to be away from home. She was no longer a little girl she had become a very fine young woman and Ethel knew it. She embraced Sally and kissed her on her cheeks and said, "Honey I love you very much. I want you to have a far better life than I had growing up. Things are changing all the time. I just want to tell you to take every opportunity to make your own life better. If your Pa wants more land to raise more crops on, that's your Pa, but you just remember, you have your own life to live. Now I know you can be a great help to Ollie."

"Thanks Ma. I love you and Pa so much. I know what you are trying to tell me. I love you even more for it," said Sally, putting her arms around her.

"Let's go ladies," hollered Jack. "It will be dark now by the time we make our rounds."

Bill was in the yard, getting another armload of wood, when he saw the Weldon's come in sight. He hurried into the house and put the wood down by the fireplace. "You've got company coming," he said to Ollie. "Guess who."

Ollie was so sore, it hurt even to try to think without it causing pain, but finally she answered, "I have no idea."

"It's Sally and her family," he replied. Ollie's eyes lit up. She loved Sally and through the years, they had shared many things together. It would be good to see her. Bill and Ed went out onto the porch, and waited for the wagon to come into the yard.

"Hi folks," said Bill, as the wagon pulled up in front of the house. "Good to see you all."

"Good to see you folks too," said Ethel, as she reached down for Ed to help her out of the wagon. Sally was next. Then Jack got down from his side of the wagon, came around, and shook hands with both of the men. Ed tied the mules to the hitching post while Bill went with the Weldon's into the house. Sally was truly shocked to see her friend in such pain. When she came to Ollie's bedside, kneeling down, she bent over her and very quietly whispered in her ear, "I love you dearly. You must get better. We have lots of things to do and to talk about," then she kissed her on the cheek.

Ollie squeezed her hand and said, "I'm trying as hard as I can to beat this."

"Well let me tell you," said Ethel, "You just might as well make up your mind to fight hard. You have more to fight for now, since you are with child, and we are here to help you." She rubbed Ollie's hand, and then said to Martha as they made their way toward the kitchen "and how have you been since little Ollie left home?"

"We all miss her very much, but, life goes on. We will always be here for her, but now she has a life of her own with Bill."

"I sure hope Jack will feel the way you folks do about your Ollie, when it comes time for our Sally to leave home. As lonely as I will be, when she does get married, I still want her to have a life of her own too," said Ethel.

"Has Sally gotten serious with somebody? Who in the world," asked Martha?

"No one that I know of, I'm just saying, I want her to have her own life." She didn't want to tell Martha right now that her daughter was sweet on her Jules. "Jack only sees the farm, crops, harvest, and more land. Do you understand what I'm trying to say?"

Martha put her arms around her and said, "Ethel, honey I went through the same thing with Ollie. We wanted her to live her own life. Even this, it could have been worse. We could have lost her and the baby. But now we have an opportunity to share our love even more with her and her whole family."

"What's got you ladies all teary eyed?" asked Jack, coming into the kitchen with Ed.

"Woman to woman talk," answered Martha.

"If it's alright with you folks, Sally came prepared to stay awhile with Ollie. She wants to help all she can," said Ethel.

"That would be wonderful. They will have so much to talk about and share all their dreams together. It will be good for Ollie," replied Martha.

"We brought lots of food from all the friends at church," said Jack. "It's in the wagon. Where would you like for me to put it?"

"Just sit it on the table," Martha replied.

Ed gave Jack a hand, helping him bring in the food. After sitting the baskets down, Jack said to Bill, "The men at church told me to tell you, not to worry about getting your crops in the ground; they were working on a plan to help you."

That seemed to please Bill very much. He knew it would be planting time soon, and with all that had happened, he had lost sight of just how soon that would be. Martha and Ethel emptied out the baskets of food on the table; there was fried chicken, collard greens, soup beans, corn bread, pickles, and some fried streak-o-lean. One basket had a chocolate cake, apple pie, and sweet potato custard in it.

Bill spoke and said, "I would like for everyone to stay and have supper with Ollie and me. This wonderful blessing is from the church family." Everyone gathered around the table as he blessed the food. After supper was over, Jack rising from the table said, "I guess we better be getting on home, there will be lots to do when we get back."

"I'll help do the dishes," said Ethel.

"No Ma, I will be glad to do them," said Sally. "This is why I wanted to come and help."

"Oh alright, you take care now, "said Ethel, as she reached out to give her daughter a hug. Jack came over, put his arms around her, and gave her a kiss. Then he went over to Ollie's bed, knelt down and kissed her hand, saying, "You will always be on my mind and in my prayers."

Everyone went outside with them, and before they got into their wagon, they shook hands and hug necks, as they said their good-byes.

Chapter Nineteen

Monday morning started out with Hershel doing some of his shenanigans. He went to his water bowl and put his hands in the water. He held them there until they were very cold. He proceeded to the bed, where Sally was sleeping. He eased up on the bed and stuck his cold hands to her face. Sally started screaming, the sound could have traveled all the way to Little River. By the time Bill got up and had his clothes on, Hershel was back in his box. Sally was petrified, standing straight up in bed with a quilt wrapped around her, not daring to move one inch.

Bill came into Sally's room trying to calm her down. "What happened?" he asked.

"I don't know. I was sleeping peaceably, when all of a sudden, I felt something ice cold touch my face and neck."

"Did you see anything?"

"Nothing, I saw nothing," replied Sally, still standing straight up in bed.

Bill went over to Hershel's box and lifted him out. Holding him up, he said, "I want you to meet Hershel, Ollie's pet raccoon. So much was going on yesterday; we forgot to tell you about him."

Sally slowly sat down in her bed. She was still shivering from the cold hands that had touched her face and was shaking with fear. She couldn't imagine what had touched her. Bill took Hershel to Ollie's bed and placed him close to her. The loud scream had awakened her too.

"You been a bad boy this morning?" she asked Hershel, as she rubbed his fur. "I don't know what I'm going to do with you. You got to behave, you can't keep scaring people."

The scream woke everyone up, including Martha. As she came into Ollie's bedroom she said, "I see you are still babying that raccoon. What are you going to do with it, when the baby comes?"

"I never gave it a thought," replied Ollie, with her eyes on Hershel.

"We got plenty of time to talk about it later," said Bill, when he saw his Ollie getting upset about the raccoon. "Right now, she doesn't need to be upset about anything."

Sally made her way into the bedroom where everyone was. Laughing, she said, but he scared me almost to death at first. I didn't know what was getting in the bed with me."

Ollie laughed too, holding her sides because of all the pain. Martha and Sally got busy cooking breakfast, while Bill headed out to the barn to milk the cow and to feed all of the animals.

"Do you think Jules will come today to see Ollie?" asked Sally, putting the biscuits on the table.

"He more than likely will. Just as soon as he can help his Pa get things done around the farm, he will light out for here," said Martha. "You seem to like Jules quite a bit."

Blushing, she said, "Jules is the only man, I've ever cared about. I'm not sure how he feels toward me; I just know how I feel about him."

"Knowing Jules, I'm sure he cares for you too."

Bill came in with the milk and set it down on the table. "Would you believe, as long as I've been milking that cow, she still paws the ground, when she runs low of feed?"

Martha took the milk, and while she was straining it, said, "I know Ollie would feel better, and maybe, even get well faster, if she knew that cow was gone from here."

"I know she probably would, but right now I can't do anything. What money we have hast to go toward getting our crop in," he replied.

———✦———

Sally was very busy, while Martha and Bill talked about the cow. She was putting everything on the table and fixing a plate for Ollie. She filled the plate with some scrambled eggs, gravy, and a biscuit filled with some of her Ma's preserves.

"I'll take her breakfast to her," said Bill, picking up the plate. As he made his way from the kitchen to Ollie's bedroom, someone was knocking on the door.

"I'll get it," said Sally, getting up from the table. When she opened the door, she almost lost her breath. It was Jules. He was surprised to see her also. For a moment, he was lost for words.

"Well, glory-be," said Martha, "we were just talking about you. Don't just stand there, come on in." Martha hugged Jules, Sally still speechless, put out her hand and shook hands with him.

"Good morning," said Jules. "Pa said he could take care of things today so I could come and see Ollie. I left early this morning. I caught a ride with Henry Beckett. He was coming down to Little River to do some fishing. How's Ollie doing?"

"Come see for yourself. She's about to have her breakfast," said Martha.

Jules followed his Ma to Ollie's bedroom, and when Ollie saw him, she began to cry.

"Hey, don't cry, do I look that bad?" said Jules, he was trying to use some humor to cheer her up.

"Oh no, you look wonderful. I'm so happy to see you, that's what made me cry," said Ollie.

Bill set the plate of food down and gave Jules a big bear hug. Jules came over, bent down, and took his time loving on his little sister. With everything that he had been told about her accident, he still wasn't prepared for what he saw. He couldn't keep from crying, even though he tried. When he gently put his arms around her, she reached up and embraced him, and they hugged and wept for a few moments.

"Breakfast is getting cold," said Martha, trying to get both of them to stop crying.

Jules stood up and wiped his eyes, then stepped aside, so Bill could help her with her breakfast. Jules came into the kitchen and sat down at the table.

"How long have you've been here?" he asked, talking to Sally.

"Pa and Ma came yesterday and I came with them to stay awhile to help Ollie and Bill. Have you had any breakfast?" Sally asked.

"No I haven't eaten yet. I wanted to get here early so I could help Bill with some of his work."

Sally sat another plate. She was so thrilled that Jules was actually sitting across the table from her; she almost dropped the plate, twice.

"Sally, do you know just how long you will be able to stay?" asked Martha.

"A few weeks I know. Pa isn't going to plant so early this year. We lost a lot of seed last year trying to get a jump on things."

When Ollie finished her breakfast, Bill brought her plate back to the kitchen, sat down with the rest, and started helping himself to breakfast. All was quiet for a little while. Sally staring at Jules, Jules not knowing what to say, and Martha was being very observant of both of them.

"What can I do to help you while I'm here?" asked Jules. He was hoping Bill had a job that would keep him there for a few days. Especially after seeing Sally was there, he wasn't in any hurry to be getting back home.

"Why don't you two take the lumber you had left and finish sealing up the cracks in the walls," suggested Martha.

"That's a good idea," replied Bill. "We can go as far as we have the material."

Jules looked at Sally, and they smiled at each other, knowing now they would be together for a few days. The sound of the work kept Ollie awake most of the day. Sally being there was good for her. She would come and sit by her bedside and they would talk for hours. Martha was pleased her Ollie had a friend that was so caring and wanted to be with her, even though, she could see Sally wanted to be close to Jules also. During the late evenings, after all the chores were finished, they gathered around Ollie's bed and would sing songs. Then each one would make up a story or some wild tale, which would keep everyone laughing. It was good to forget about the accident for a while and be happy and light-hearted.

Hershel had made friends with Sally and when she was sitting down he would come and sit beside her, and at times, he would hop up in her lap and sit a spell. Ollie was pleased her little friend had someone to show him some love and attention.

The lumber was gone and most of the cracks were too. It had taken a few days to do the work and it was getting time for Jules to be heading back home. He had enjoyed being with them, sharing the bed with Bill on his new straw-tick mattress. Sally was sharing the other bed with Martha. At the breakfast table, he made the announcement he would haft to be leaving, he needed to start home this morning so he could help his Pa.

Martha wasn't too surprised. She knew her son well enough to know that he wouldn't leave all the work for his Pa to do.

Sally was sad, but she too, knew he had to go. Jules went in and sat down with Ollie. He reached out, took her long black hair, and gently pulled it through his fingers. "Little one, I've got to go home now. Pa probably has been standing on his head since I've been gone." They both laughed, knowing their Pa was taking good care of everything. Jules bent over, kissed Ollie, and then went back to the kitchen.

"Ma, Ma," called Ollie.

"Yes dear," answered Martha, coming into her room rather quickly.

"What is it dear? Are you hurting?" she asked.

"No, I'm doing alright. The pain isn't as severe as it has been. I was thinking about Pa. I know when Bill is away, I miss him something awful. I'm just laying here trying to get better. There is nothing anyone to do for me that will help me heal any faster. I haven't talked it over with Bill, so I don't know how he will feel at what I'm about to say." Bill and Sally had followed Martha into Ollie's room. He was listening to her every word.

"Sally has told me she was going to stay with me at least two weeks, so I was just thinking why don't you go home with Jules and be with Pa. Planting time is just around the corner, and I'm sure he has a thousand questions he wants to ask you, as he always does this time of year."

"But honey, you're not even sitting up yet," said Martha.

"I know, but as soon as I feel, I can do it, I will. Everyone has been so kind to me going out of their way to help me. Healing is from God, and as quickly as He heals me, I will be out of this bed doing for myself. It's been close to two weeks and I'm already moving a little bit."

"What do you think Bill?" asked Martha.

"Whatever Ollie feels, she is the only one who knows how, and when, she can move and sit up. Sally and I can take care of her, if you want to go with Jules. You all can come back on the weekends, if that is what you would want to do," said Bill.

"Ma, I will be coming every weekend for a while to help Bill in the fields, you and Pa can come with me," said Jules.

"Ollie, are you sure about this?" asked Martha.

"I want you to go and be with Pa and help him and Jules. I remember how it is this time of year there on the farm. I will be all right. There is not anything, anyone can do for me to speed up my healing. It will take time. I feel bad having everyone just waiting here with me for the healing to happen."

"Right now, since there's nothing no one can do, but wait, if you wanted to go home with Jules, yaw can use my wagon and take one of the mules. When yaw come back next weekend you can bring the mule and wagon back then," said Bill.

"I'll take good care of her if you want to go. I came to stay a few weeks. We are not going to plant as early this year, so I've got time to help with Ollie," said Sally.

"I think the little one is right. Ma, you know how independent she is. You might as well come along with me and enjoy my company," said Jules, laughing.

"Well, alright, but I will be back this weekend. We'll see how it goes," replied Martha. While she was getting her things together, Bill was hitching up the mule to the wagon. Jules walked back to the kitchen with Sally, he was very slow to say anything. When he did say something, it didn't come out just right.

He said, "I'll kiss you every day . . . No, No, that's not what I was trying to say. I was going to say, I will miss you every day," as he dropped his head down with embarrassment.

Sally couldn't help herself. She walked over and kissed Jules very lightly on his lips. He put his arms around her and said, "I will miss you." They walked out onto the porch together waiting for Martha to say good-bye. Finally, they were all ready to go. Jules climbed aboard and Bill helped Martha up. Jules spoke a soft word of giddy-up to the mule and they headed toward home.

———————✦———————

Sally was busy in the kitchen fixing breakfast along with cooking some things for dinner. She knew this was a big weekend for her. Jules was coming to help Bill do some plowing and she was so excited. She was trying not to show her feelings so much outwardly. Ollie had managed to turn a little bit on her side. She would rest in that position until the pain became so unbearable, then she would alternate positions several times a day. Sally bathed her every morning, while Bill did the outside chores. Ollie was so happy that Sally was with her. She knew though the time was getting close for her to go home.

Bill came in with the milk pail filled with milk. He sat it down on the table and went to see Ollie. "How are things? Did you rest good last night?" he asked.

"I had a better night than I've had these past three weeks. How is the cow this morning?" she asked.

"Still ornery as ever, she hasn't changed one little bit. Honey, I'm so sorry I let this happened to you. I can never forgive myself for not listening to you about the little heifer."

"You've got to stop blaming yourself. It's done, it's over. We must make the best of things. I love you, and we will make it together."

Bill knelt down beside her and very gently put his arms around her, held her for a moment, kissing her tenderly, and with a whisper, said, "I love you so much." He was shocked to hear a knock on the door. Before he could even rise to his feet, Sally was already there.

"Come in," she said.

"Good morning," said Jules, as he touched her hand. "Looks like you got things going in the kitchen."

"Good morning," said Bill, as he came over to shake hands with him. "How are things at home?"

"They're good. We got most of the upland plowed. Pa wants to start planting by the end of April. How's my little sister doing this morning?" he asked Ollie, as he entered her bedroom?

"I'm much better. I've been turning on my sides some. I'm trying to get where I will be able to sit up in the next couple of weeks. Just lying flat on my back all the time has just about done me in." He knelt down and kissed her on her cheeks.

"Ma and Pa said to tell you they will be here next weekend. Several of the farmers are coming to help you folks. The way everyone was talking, it wouldn't surprise me at all, if they didn't get all your land ready for planting next weekend."

Sally called, "Breakfast is ready, and you men get washed up, while I bring Ollie a plate." Hershel had gotten close to Sally. He really did enjoy all her petting, rubbing, and holding him. He followed her throughout the house. When she brought Ollie's breakfast, he jumped upon the bed, and lay down beside her. Ollie took the time to rub his fur and pet him a little, but when Sally went back to the kitchen, he hopped off the bed and followed her. Ollie knew she had lost her Hershel to Sally. Being bedridden, it was just as well. She knew it would be a very long time before she could play with him, if ever.

Bill fixed his plate, picked it up and said, "Excuse me and I will have breakfast with Ollie this morning." That was all right with Sally and Jules for they would enjoy being alone.

Chapter Twenty

Many of the farmers did come the next Saturday to help Bill get his land ready for planting. They brought their plows and used their mules and horses to plow up the land. The women folks came bringing plenty of food to fix for the men. The men were in the fields working, by the time the sun came up over the horizon. Since many of the farmers lived so far away, they would haft to quit working around four o'clock in the afternoon, so they could get ready to start home. Even though the farmers were very tired, they still took time to enjoy a good meal, and listen to the music, Eddie Long and Harris Elrod played for them, before they headed for home. The weather was very helpful and cooperative in that it didn't rain until the seeds were planted.

It was now May 1, and Sally would have to leave for home this weekend. She really didn't want to leave, but she knew her folks were depending on her. She needed to go home to help them with the planting of their crops. Saturday morning had arrived. She had put all her things together, getting ready to go home. Her family was coming this morning to get her. She had tears in her eyes as she brought Ollie her breakfast.

"I will miss you so much," said Ollie. "You have been so good to me, to help me, to feed and bathe me. I'll never forget your kindness," as she reached up to hug Sally.

"I just wish I could stay longer, but you know how things have to be. If Pa doesn't get his seed in the ground pretty quick, there won't be any need to plant anything this year."

"I know," said Ollie. "What happened to me couldn't have come at a worse time. We were just getting started with our lives as husband and wife, and our first year with the farm. Everyone has been so good to us. I will miss you so much. I have a request of you, and if you don't want to do it or you think your folks wouldn't want you to do it, just say no and I will understand."

"What in the world can I do for you?" asked Sally.

"I want you to take Hershel with you when you leave. He has taken a liking to you and I can't move about and take care of him. He loves someone to pet him and rub his fur occasionally. He follows you everywhere you go and makes every step you make."

"Oh, Ollie, sure I will take him, but are you really sure you want me to?"

"I'm sure. Bill and I have talked about it. With him in the field, and me not able to get around very much, it would be a blessing if you could take him."

"Then it's settled. Hershel can go with me. I know it will be all right with Ma and Pa. I just know it. I once had a pet squirrel that Pa brought home with him from one of his hunting trips. They like to pet the animals too."

"Well, it looks like your folks are coming down the road," said Bill, coming in from doing the milking. "I can see a wagon coming."

Sally set her things out on the porch and got Hershel ready for traveling. She put him in his box and closed the lid. Bill had made the box for him to travel in. She set the box next to her things, and went back to Ollie's bedside. She found her in tears. She put her arms around her and softly said, "I'll take special care of Hershel, don't you worry yourself about him."

"I'm not crying, because he is going home with you, I'm crying, because you are leaving. I'm gonna miss you something awful," Ollie replied.

After straining the milk and putting it away, Bill left Sally and Ollie alone, and went out on the front porch to greet the Weldon's when they got there. He came back into the house quickly, saying, "It's not your folks. It's the Greens coming." He went back out on the porch, so he could greet them.

"Good morning Carl, Edna, and Dianne. We thought you all were the Weldon's coming," said Bill.

"Good morning Bill," said the Green family, all speaking at the same time. "We aren't the Weldon's, but we have come to help out again. We talked to Jack and Ethel last Sunday at church. When they said they needed Sally back home to help with the planting, we decided that Dianne can take Sally's place, and stay with Ollie for a while, if it's alright with you?"

"If it's alright, it's more than alright. I wasn't real sure how I was going to work in the fields and watch after Ollie. You are a God sent blessing," said Bill, helping the women down from the wagon.

They no more got on the porch, when Bill looked up the road, and this time, it was the Weldon's coming. The Green family made their way on into the house, and was welcomed by Sally and Ollie.

"How are you doing?" Edna asked, taking Ollie by her hand.

"I'm able to move some. I've been turning a little on my side each day. It still hurts something terrible."

"Hello Ollie," spoke Dianne. "I've come to relieve Sally. I hope you don't mind."

"Lord no. Bill and I need all the help we can get for a while." Ollie reached up and gave her a big hug.

You could hear Bill greeting the Weldon's when they came into the yard. Ethel came on in the house, leaving Jack outside to talk about farming with Bill. She hugged her daughter, and then went over and gathered around Ollie's bed with Dianne.

"You're looking much better than the last time I saw you. How are you feeling dear?" asked Ethel.

"Much better than I was, I'm able to move about some. Sally has really been a great help to me. She has done everything in the house. You have a wonderful daughter, and I have a great friend."

"Well, thank you dear. I guess we best be going. Jack promised the pastor he would help them work at the church today."

Sally made her way over to Ollie's side and hugged her for a long time. With tears in her eyes, she whispered in her ear, "I love you."

"Come on girls, we've got lots to do today," said Jack, as he came to the door of Ollie's room, tipping his hat at her, it was his way of saying hello and good-bye.

Bill helped Ethel and Sally up on the wagon, and put Sally's things in the back, along with the box with Hershel in it. He stood waving at them till they were out of sight.

———◆———

Ollie was sitting up some and trying her best not to be a burden on anyone. Her family was coming for the weekend and she wanted to be able to sit up some, while they were there. Bill had removed the pine straw from the flowers around the house and barn. Everything was beginning to break out and look like spring. You could just feel the wonderful feeling of life, as you saw the flowers blooming, trees budding, and the grass getting greener each day.

Dianne was a wonderful helper as Sally had been; she was able to encourage Ollie and help keep her spirit up. Ollie was doing her best to move as much as she could. The baby was now moving in her womb, and this was encouraging her to try harder to move about. She hadn't told anyone about the baby moving yet. She wanted to make sure it wasn't just her bones trying to heal in her body. She still missed Hershel jumping up on her bed, and sticking his nose underneath her covers every morning. Nevertheless, she knew Sally loved him and was taking good care of him.

It would be a couple of months before Ollie could sit up completely. Dr. Sands had been faithful to come every week, but now he was only coming once a month. Bill's parents came every other weekend, alternating with Ollie's parents. They all were very loving and helpful, and encouraged them greatly with their support. This was the weekend for Ollie's parents to come. They were there by the time the sun came up over the mountain. Ed worked in the fields with Bill, while Martha helped Dianne with the house chores.

Bill worked hard in the fields and as he worked; Ollie was always on his mind. She was beginning to make progress in getting around, but as she moved about, she stooped over to keep from pulling her ribs apart. The ribs were healing in the broken position, so it was forcing Ollie to bend forward, creating a bow in her back. She was healing, and she was getting better, but she would never be the same.

At noon, Bill and Ed came in from the fields for dinner. "Hello darling," said Bill. "You sure look great. I'm so proud of you. You've come through hell and back, you're my angel."

"Oh Bill, I love you. I love you," she replied.

They sat down, Bill, Ed, Martha, Dianne, and Ollie in her make shift chair at the end of the table. Bill had made the chair especially for her. He made it so it would fit her body, and then she could sit with them at the table. They said Grace, and began eating.

"Ma," said Ollie, with a pause in her words, "I know Pa and Jules need you at home. It's hard for them to be doing what all four of us used to do, tending to all the livestock, and working in the fields. I can make it now with just Bill and myself. Dianne is going home tomorrow. You all, with

Bill's parents, have helped me get this far, and now; I think it's time for me to start doing things for myself. I've got to start or I will never do it"

"Well honey, if you are sure about it, when your father finishes helping Bill this weekend, we'll plan to come maybe, once a month to help out. How about that?" asked Martha. She knew it would be good for her to start doing things for herself and Bill. She also knew Ollie wanted to find her own way back. Everything was going to be completely different now, from the easiest task to the most difficult.

"Ollie, are you sure?" asked Ed.

"Yes. The baby is due somewhere around the last of August or early September, and I'll need Ma then," she replied.

Ed managed to get alone for some man-to-man talk with Bill.

"Bill, I appreciate you for the way you have taken care of our Ollie. I know it has been hard for the both of you."

"I love Ollie so much. I should have listened to her about the cow. I can never forgive myself for leaving her alone to milk her. She was scared of the cow and didn't want me to buy her anyway."

"Well that's all in the past now, we must do all we can for her now and go forward," replied Ed.

Sunday morning found Ed and Martha in the kitchen fixing breakfast for all of them. Bill was down at the barn taking care of the livestock and milking the cow. Dianne was putting her things together to be ready to go, when her parents came to get her. After breakfast, Bill helped Ed hitch up his horses to the wagon. Martha took Ollie in her arms and holding her close to her breast she said, "Honey you're going to be just fine. I'll be back in a few weeks. However, if you need me before then, just send Bill. I'll come running." She gathered up all her belongings and headed out the door.

"Dianne, I want to thank you for helping our Ollie. May the good Lord bless you and all the rest, for being so kind to help Ollie and Bill."

"Thank you ma'am, it was something I wanted to do for them," she replied.

Ed and Martha left Bill, Ollie, and Dianne on the porch, waving to them as they headed for home.

It was around noon when Dianne saw her folks coming down the road. She was out in the yard sweeping with a brush broom. She was glad to see them. Her two brothers couldn't wait for the wagon to stop. They were already out of the wagon and hugging their sister before it ever came to a standstill. They were so pleased to see one another. Bill came out of the house and helped Edna down, while Carl tied up the mules. Right off, the men started talking about farm stuff, while Edna made her way to the porch to speak to Ollie.

"How are you doing?" asked Edna, after setting down her bag. "I see you're sitting up and moving about some."

"I'm doing some better. I can feel my bones trying to heal. They make all kind of sounds in my body," Ollie replied.

Edna started feeling of her stomach. "Have you felt the baby move yet?" she asked.

"Yes. It's moving quite a bit now. I haven't told Bill yet, I wanted to talk to Ma or you about it first. I didn't want him to worry about me with all he has been doing."

"Well, I think it's time for you to tell Bill everything that's going on with you. He needs to know, so he can prepare himself for it," said Edna. "I'm going to fix dinner for all of us. I brought some good vegetable soup and I will cook some corn bread with some pork meat. How does that sound to you?"

"Wonderful, just wonderful," Ollie replied.

It was late in the evening when the Green's headed for home. The boys were still picking at Dianne as they headed down the road.

<hr/>

Now that Ollie and Bill were alone, they were not sure how to act. People had surrounded them for the past few months. They were taking a rest on the front porch. Bill was leaning against the post of the porch, while Ollie was resting in the homemade chair he had made for her. She was the first one to speak.

"Bill, I should have told you about me being with child. I was waiting to talk to Ma just to make sure I wasn't just feeling bad."

"Honey, let's not talk about that anymore. You've been through too much already; let's just concentrate on you continuing to get better and the baby, that will be coming soon."

"That's what I'm trying to say. The baby is moving. I can feel it ever so often, especially at night, when everything is quiet and I'm lying on my right side."

Bill stood up and started dancing a little jig, clapping his hands, and he yelled, "We're gonna have a boy, we're gonna have a boy." After he settled down some, he turned to Ollie and said, "You're the strongest and bravest woman I know."

"I love you Bill Franklin, and just for you, I pray the baby will be a boy."

"I've got some good news for you too," said Bill, putting his arms around her. "I got an offer from Paul Crow, he wants to swap us a smaller cow for our cow, what do you think about that?"

"That's great, just great. I always wanted a smaller cow. Thank you, Bill. What is Paul going to do with our cow?"

"He wants to use her for breeding. Since our cow gives as much milk as she does, Paul thinks if he can breed her, he will eventually get some little heifers that will give lots of milk too." Bill took Ollie in his arms very gently, kissing her, as they made their way back into the house.

Paul came on Monday, arriving around noon. Ollie was sitting on the porch, in her special chair, enjoying the scenery of the flowers and taking in the aroma of the fresh blossoms on the fruit trees. Bill was coming in from the fields where he had been working. She had watched the wagon as it came down the dusty road. Paul had the smaller cow tied to the back of the wagon. It was a mix between a White face Hereford and a Guernsey. When Ollie saw the cow, she knew she was going to be very pleased with the trade. They said this cow was so gentle; she would let you milk her without any feed in the trough.

"Good afternoon Ollie," said Paul. "How's things been for you?"

"Much better now, thank you." Ollie was, what would you say, moon struck, by the little heifer. She managed to get to her feet and stood up holding on to the post of the porch. She wanted so much to step down, and put her hands on the heifer.

"Howdy Paul," said Bill, as he approached him. "I see you made it today."

"I wanted to get here a little earlier, but the children wanted to come to town and hang out there, till I came back through. Waiting for them to get things together took a little longer than it should have," said Paul. "Inez and Ron have got the dancing fever. Ever since New Year's Eve, they have been working on that new dance. The one the folks from Atlanta taught them. Lot of the young folks is meeting in town today, just to dance. Can you believe that?"

"Well that's good," replied Ollie. "The young folks need something to do besides planting and gathering throughout the year."

Paul untied the heifer and brought her to the porch. Ollie took her time, and slowly made her way over to the edge of the porch, and then she was able to touch the little heifer on its head. The heifer raised her head and licked her hand. It was as if to say, 'hello', to Ollie.

"It will take me a little while to get the cow from the pasture. You can sit and talk with Ollie or go with me to get the cow," said Bill.

"If you don't mind I'll stay here and keep Ollie Company while you're gone. I haven't had the pleasure of visiting with her," replied Paul.

"Good enough. I'll get back as soon as I can," he said, as he headed for the pasture.

Paul sat down on the porch close to Ollie. It seemed hard for him to start talking to her, but finally he said, "Ollie, when I heard the news at church about your accident, I cried for hours. I've prayed for you every day. I thought how hard it would be, if it were my Inez going through what you have been through. I couldn't help, but cry and pray."

She reached over, and touched him on his shoulder, and with tears in her eyes, she said, "Paul, you will never know what this means to me. Knowing someone like you has taken the time to pray for me is awesome. Your children must be very proud of you."

"I'm a little worried about Inez and Ron. Ever since they learned the new dance at the New Year's Eve celebration, they keep talking about going to Atlanta to learn more."

"Well, since I can't do very much around the house and nothing in the fields, I can at least help you pray for your children," said Ollie.

"Thanks Ollie," Paul said, as he put his hand over hers.

They could see that Bill was almost back to the barn with the cow. Paul stood up, patted Ollie on her back, and headed for the barn. The cow was very much upset, having to come in from the pasture this time of day. She was snorting from her nose and jerking her head up and down, trying to get loose from Bill.

"You said she was an unruly cow," said Paul, as he got close to Bill. "With the plans I have in mind for her, it won't matter how mad she gets."

"Thanks Paul. I appreciate what you are doing. I know Ollie will be more than pleased."

"Ever since the pastor told the church what had happened to Ollie, I've wanted to do something to help. This is my way of helping you," replied Paul. "I better be getting along. My children will be wondering what happened to their Pa." He took the rope; Bill had around the neck of the cow, and led her to the back of the wagon. Even while he was tying her to the wagon, she was trying to butt him. He climbed up on the wagon, tipped his hat to Ollie, and said to Bill, "Don't you worry any; me and this cow are going to get along just fine."

Chapter Twenty-One

Ollie accepted the fact she would always have a bowed back, but as long as she had Bill to love her, and could have a family that was all she needed. Tom and Mattie, and Ed, Martha, and Jules, alternated coming on the weekends so they could help her and Bill. The men helped Bill with the farm work with Saturdays being the main workday. The women did the chores in and around the house, and talked much about the soon coming baby. It was a joyful time. Ollie was now eight months pregnant, and she was able to move around more and do light housework with less pain. She had heard from all the women, what you should do to help the baby be born. All the different kind of tricks, how you must lay, sit, walk about, work, don't work, exercise, don't exercise, she felt as if she had it all down pat.

Things were looking good on the farm. With all the help they were getting, Bill and Ollie were very pleased with how everything was coming along. There was a good stand of cotton and each stem was loaded with cotton bolls. The corn was producing just as well. It looked as if every stalk had two ears of corn on them. If things kept going as they were, they would have a great harvest.

Things were settling down around the farm now, since it was lay-by time. Bill was busy keeping things repaired around the place. One of the jobs, he wanted to do, was make sure he repaired the roof of the house. He wanted the old house to be warm and dry this winter for Ollie and the baby. After repairing every spot he could find on the roof, he got busy cutting wood for the winter months. The days and weeks were slipping right on by. Neither one was paying too much attention to how quickly time was passing. He would take the mules with the sled and go to the woods to cut down trees. He would cut up the limbs and logs for firewood, but he always made sure, he didn't get very far from the house.

Ollie was keeping herself busy making baby clothes. She had learned how to sew by watching her mother make their clothes. She was able to move about slowly through the house with the help of a cane. She was trying to be as useful as she could. The baby was pushing hard against her ribs now, causing her much pain and making it difficult to breathe. She never let on to Bill. Every day, week after week, the pain was becoming almost unbearable. As the baby grew, her breathing was more painful, so she took every moment she could, to lie down and rest. She did her resting, while Bill was working outside, she didn't want him to worry about her.

She could hear Bill's axe as he made heavy strokes, cutting up some of the logs he had brought into the yard. When he heard Ollie cry out, he dropped everything, stumbling over the wood, he ran, almost falling up the steps into the house.

"It's coming, Bill, the baby's coming," screamed Ollie, as she tried to get to the door.

"Let me help you to the bed. I've got to go get Edna, can you hold out till I fetch her?"

"I'll try, but you better not waste any time doing it."

He eased her down on the bed and covered her with some quilts. He ran to the barn as fast as he could to get the mule. He hitched the mule to the wagon, and headed for the Green's farm. Away he went as fast as the mule would go. By the time, the wagon stopped in their yard, he was on the porch yelling for Mrs. Green.

"It's Ollie isn't it?" said Mrs. Green, taking off her apron when she saw Bill at the door.

"Yes, the baby is coming. I need you to come now."

Carl came in from the backyard and he heard the news about Ollie, so he said, "Bill, you and Edna take our wagon with my fresh horses and go on. I'll come behind you with your mule and wagon."

Bill didn't take time to answer. He helped Carl hitch up the horses to the wagon, while Edna was getting her medical bag. Edna kissed Carl and told him to be careful. She and Bill headed back to his home, hoping and praying that everything was all right. They could hear Ollie screaming and crying, as they got near the house. The baby was very close to being born, and Edna knew they needed to hurry with their preparations for the birth of the baby.

"Bill, get the fire going, and heat plenty of water. I'll take care of Ollie and the baby," said Edna. She opened her bag and took out everything she thought she would need for the delivery.

———•❖•———

Bill was working as fast as he could in the kitchen, when he heard the sound of the wagon come into the yard. Carl didn't bother to knock; he came straight into the house. "How's she doing," he asked?

"Good I hope. Edna wanted me to get the fire going and heat some water," Bill replied.

Carl sat down and pulled out his pipe. He packed it with tobacco and lit it up. Bill was as nervous as he could be. He spilt more water, as he tried to fill the kettle, than he was getting in it. He walked around the table one way and then the other. Carl didn't make a move from where he first sat down. He had been through this three times already, so he was amused watching Bill. As he picked up the kettle, checking to see if the water was hot, he almost dropped it, when he heard the sound of the baby crying. He put the kettle back on the stove and quickly ran to the bedroom.

"It's a boy," said Edna, holding the small infant wrapped in a blanket close to her. Bill looked at the baby and with a smile; he knelt down by Ollie's bed.

"Honey, you did great. I love you, I love you."

Ollie smiled. Edna put the baby in her arms and asked Bill, "How about that warm water?"

Bill made haste back to the kitchen. When he returned, he had the kettle filled with hot water and a wash pan.

"Now leave us alone for a little while," said Edna. As Bill left the room, she got busy cleaning up the baby and giving Ollie a good cloth bath. The baby's tiny stomach was telling him, he was hungry. As Ollie took the baby to her bosom, she felt peace, embarrassment, joy, excitement, and many more sensations were running through her body as the baby began to nurse. While the baby was nursing, she realized she was hungry too. "Isn't he so beautiful?" she asked.

Bill, smiling from ear to ear, with a little dance in his step, went back into the kitchen to check on some more hot water. He grabbed Carl and together they danced a little jig around the kitchen table.

"Ollie you did just fine, the baby is a healthy little boy, and you delivered him all right. I'm sure you and Bill will be able have many, many, more children," said Edna.

"You think so? Do you really think Bill will love me again with my body like it is? With my chest pushed in and my back bowed. I just hope the shape my body is in, doesn't turn him away from loving me," said Ollie.

"Don't you ever say things like that? Bill loved you before the accident, and even more now. Just you wait and see."

Bill returned from the kitchen and said, "Ollie, honey, what are we going to name our baby? I haven't given it a thought till now."

She replied, "I have thought for a long time about a name for our baby, if it was a boy, I thought about Homer? That was my grandpa's name."

"That's all right with me."

"Well that's not all his name. It will be "Homer William Franklin," said Ollie.

"We've got to let our folks know about the baby," said Bill.

"I know," replied Ollie. "Ma will be so happy, but she wanted to be here when it came though."

"Bill, if it's alright with you, I can tell both your parents tomorrow about the baby. I'm going to Dawsonville to buy some supplies and I would be more than glad to go by and tell them the good news. I can tell Dr. Sands also," said Carl.

"Carl, that's plumb good of you to do that," said Bill.

"We had already talked about ways to help you children when the baby came. This could be one of them," said Edna. "I'm going to stay with you till your folks come."

"I better be getting back and help with all of the chores," said Carl. "I'll come back, day after tomorrow and get you," he said as he kissed Edna bye.

Ollie had a good night's sleep. The baby rested good, only crying when he was hungry. It had been a long time since she could breathe as well as she was breathing now. She still had a lot of pain, but when she looked at little Homer putting his small hands in his mouth, twitching his nose, she was convinced every bit of the pain was worth it. She kept the baby close to her side. Edna was relieved that the baby and Ollie were doing so well. She praised the Lord for the miracle He had given them.

Bill was so excited, that when he went to milk the cow, he sang all the way to the barn. He patted the little heifer on her back as he started milking her. It seemed all the livestock was enjoying the moment with him. This was a great day for him! He told all the animals about his son, Homer. He couldn't help himself. He felt so happy and blessed. When he came back into the house, he was still singing and clicking his heels. Ollie had never seen him this happy.

Sitting up in bed, she said, "Did you find a pot of gold out there this morning?"

"Not out there. My treasure is right here in this house. You and little Homer is my pot of gold." He came over, kissed her, and took the baby up in his arms saying, "Welcome to your home little fella." Homer looked lost in his father's hands. Bill held him in one hand and with the other; he touched the baby's face ever so gently with one of his large fingers.

Edna was on top of things. She had given Ollie a bath along with the baby and was now in the kitchen fixing dinner. It made her happy to see Bill making over Ollie and the baby the way he was. The sound of a wagon coming into the yard brought more excitement to the household. They all knew it would be either Ollie's folks or Bill's. He handed the baby back to Ollie and went outside to greet whoever it was. It was Bill's family.

"Good morning, Grandma and Grandpa," said Bill, with the sound of joy and laughter in his voice, as he helped his Ma down from the wagon.

"Those words has a wonderful sound to them," said Mattie as she hugged Bill. "Congratulations. How's everyone doing?"

"Just fine, just fine," said Bill as he reached out to shake hands with his Pa. Tom never took Bill's hand, but embraced him with a big bear hug, saying, "Son, I'm mighty proud of you and Ollie. Now let's go inside and see our grandson."

Edna was holding the baby when they came in. Ollie was setting up in the bed, trying to make herself as comfortable as possible. She was still in so much pain.

"Would you like to hold your grandson?" asked Edna, holding the baby out to Mattie.

Mattie took the baby and pressed her lips against his little cheeks. Little Homer seemed to know how much he was being loved. He would smile each time someone would speak to him or kiss him.

"Tom, take a good look at your grandson," said Mattie while uncovering him, so he could get a better look at little Homer.

Tom took his pipe out of his mouth and laid it on the table next to Ollie's bed. He stared for the longest moment at the small infant. Finally, he got enough nerve to reach out and take the baby in his arms. Holding it close to him, he didn't know what to say to the baby. When the words finally came out of his mouth, he was embarrassed with himself, because he asked, "How you feeling little fella?" knowing the baby couldn't answer him back.

"How are you doing Ollie?" asked Tom, handing the baby back to Mattie.

"Much better now, thank you," she replied.

"We are so happy for you," said Mattie. "Carl came by this morning telling us how well you did, and how beautiful the baby was. He was right."

The women folks were enjoying themselves, talking about the baby, and how well Ollie did in giving birth. While Tom and Bill went outside to talk men talk, but mostly about how well Ollie and the farm were doing. As evening came, they all enjoyed the wonderful supper Mattie and Edna had prepared. Bill had put his homemade bed in the other bedroom, with the new bed he bought. He was using it for all the folks to sleep on that came to help them. He slept on a pallet next to Ollie's bed. When little Homer cried out during the night, he woke up everyone. By morning, they all were happy the baby had decided to sleep a little late. Ollie had managed to turn over on her side and she was facing Bill. She watched him as he lay on the floor next to her, and then she reached out her hand and touched his face. He was startled for a moment, until he realized it was her touching him. He took her hand in his, kissed it several times and spoke in a low whisper to her, "Ollie, you will never know just how much I love you."

Before she could say a word, someone dropped a pan in the kitchen, which caused her to quickly turn and look in that direction. It was Mattie. She was trying to start breakfast without waking anyone; she came to the door and apologized saying, "I'm so sorry."

Edna made her way to the kitchen. She wanted to help Mattie with breakfast. Bill was on his feet immediately. He knew he needed to take care of his chores outside. As he went outside, and started to step off the porch, there was Tom coming from the barn with the milk pail in his hand. He said, "I thought while you all were sleeping, I would take care of things outside."

"Thanks Pa," said Bill reaching out to take the milk pail. "What do you think about the little heifer?"

"She shore is gentle. Ollie will certainly be pleased to milk her."

Tears rolled down Bill's cheeks as he stepped back up on the porch. "The little heifer is so gentle you can milk her without feeding her. Why in the world didn't I listen to Ollie about the small heifer in town? I could have saved her all this agony and pain. I wanted the one that gave more milk; she wanted the one that was so gentle. It's my fault that Ollie is like she is today. Oh God," prayed Bill," why didn't I listen to her?"

"Son, you've got to stop blaming yourself," said Tom, putting his arms around him. "No one wanted this to happen, but it did. It is done. You have to continue to be brave through this. She mustn't see you like this. Ollie is handling all this very well. Be strong for her sake."

Bill wiped his eyes, and thanked his Pa for the sound advice. Then they went into the kitchen where Mattie and Edna had just set a big breakfast on the table.

———◆———

It was such a pleasant day; everyone was enjoying it very much. Ollie was sitting up in bed, holding little Homer. Edna and Mattie were through with dinner and cleaning up the kitchen. Bill and Tom were walking through the fields looking at the corn and cotton. Tom had his pipe going, and was enjoying a good smoke. Bill, as he looked down the road, turned to his Pa and said, "I see dust stirring up down the road, it might be Ollie's Ma and Pa coming. I guess we better be getting back to the house."

Surprisingly, they beat the visitor to the house. It wasn't Ollie's parents. It was Dr. Sands. When he drove his buggy into the yard, they were waiting to greet him.

"Howdy men," said Dr. Sands, as he tried to brush some of the dust off his coat. "It was a mighty dusty trip down here this time." Stepping down from the wagon, he asked, "How's our little woman doing? I bet her and the baby are glad it's over."

"They are doing fine. Come on in and see for yourself." Bill replied.

Tom knocked out what tobacco he had left in his pipe and followed them into the house. He found Mattie in the kitchen; Edna was with Ollie and the baby.

Tom said, "not hurrying you none, but don't you think when Ollie's parents get here, we best be getting back to our place. We live close enough that we can come back every so often and check on them, what do you think?"

"I guess you're right. That's your Grandson you are talking about though," replied Mattie.

"I know, but there is just so little room in this house. She needs Edna now more than any of us, that's what I'm saying."

"Well, little woman, I see you have brought a fine young man into the world," said Dr. Sands, as he picked up the baby. He looked Homer over real good and checked him out from head to toe. "The baby is just fine. What did you folks call him?"

"We named him Homer William Franklin," said Ollie.

"That's a good name for a boy like this one," Dr. Sands replied. "Now let's have a good look at you." After checking Ollie out thoroughly, he was pleased at what he found. Other than all her broken bones that had healed in the bent position, she was doing just great.

"Ollie, what I've got to tell you isn't going to be good news. I've been to Atlanta, and talked to all the new doctors they have down there, about your case. After much discussion, they have all agreed, there is no way to reconstruct your ribs correctly to your spine. With your sternum bone pushed as far back as it is, they are afraid with more movement of the ribs, it could puncture your lungs, heart, or injure your spine, even causing paralysis, maybe, for life. Ollie, I'm so sorry."

"Right now, I'm the happiest woman around. I have a fine husband that loves me, a beautiful baby boy, and a house full of loved ones and friends," said Ollie.

"That's real good Ollie. With an attitude like you have, you will be blessed for years to come," Dr. Sands replied. "I better be going. It will be very late when I get back to town. I want to stop by and see how Mr. Beckett is doing. Some says he has come down with a very bad cold. We can't have the only blacksmith in town laid up for a while. Ollie, please try to take it as easy as you can. You have a long way to go and it won't be easy for you. You can do it, but you must take one day at a time. Unless you need me before then, I won't be back until the end of the month."

"Thank you Doctor for everything," said Ollie, shaking his hand.

Bill and Tom walked the Doctor to his buggy, shook hands with him, and watched as he rode back up the road.

Chapter Twenty-Two

It was about four in the evening when Bill saw something else coming down the road. He couldn't make out right away what it was. It looked like one of those wagons, covered with canvas, just like the ones they used in the wagon drives going out west. As it got closer, he finally recognized it was Big John and Belle pulling the wagon. By now, everyone was on the porch, except Ollie, waiting to see what in the world was coming.

"Hello everybody," yelled Ed from the wagon, as it rolled to a stop in the yard. Martha looked like she was holding on to the wagon for dear life. Bill was the first one off the porch and into the yard. He reached up, and helped Martha down, while Tom held the horses steady. By the time she was on the ground, Ed was off the wagon, and was already shaking hands with the men.

Martha gave Bill a big hug and asked, "How are Ollie and the baby doing?"

"Fine," Bill replied. "Come on in." He helped her up on the porch. Ed and Tom followed behind them.

"Well, would you just look at that? Isn't this the prettiest little thing you've ever seen," said Martha, taking little Homer from Ollie's arms. She held him close and kissed him repeatedly. She handed him over to Grandpa Number 2.

"You're right," replied Ed. "He is a beautiful baby." He held him while Martha gave hugs and kisses to Ollie.

"Did you do alright giving birth to the baby?"

"She did great. Ollie was a little trooper through it all," said Edna, before Ollie could answer her Ma.

"Oh Edna, I was so pleased to hear you were here to help her. Thank you, thank you so much," said Martha moving close to her and giving her a big hug.

Ed, handing the baby to Bill, knelt down by Ollie's bed and very gently took his daughter in his arms and said, "I love you honey. I don't know what I would do without you. It's hard enough, you being this far away."

Ollie put her small hands on her Pa's face and said, "Pa, I miss you too. Don't worry. I'm going to be fine. You'll see."

"Well, you got to close your eyes now. I brought you something, but you can't see it till I bring it into the house."

"Need help?" asked Bill, handing the baby back to Martha.

"Yep, I could use some," he replied. The men followed Ed out to the wagon.

"I saw your wagon coming down the road and for the life of me; I couldn't make out what it was for a while. What do you have covered up under there anyway?" asked Bill.

"It's something I've been working on all summer," replied Ed. He pulled the cover off, and Tom and Bill was truly surprised. Underneath the cover were a beautiful baby bed and a rocking cradle that he had made for the baby. It was all hand crafted and so beautiful. Bill and Ed took the baby bed, while Tom brought in the cradle, and they sat them down next to Ollie's bed. Everybody gathered around, waiting for Ed to tell Ollie when to open her eyes.

"We're ready," he said. "Now open your eyes."

When Ollie opened her eyes and saw the baby bed and cradle, she was speechless, and then she started to cry. "It's beautiful Pa, just beautiful. When in the world did you have time to do something like this?"

"Late nights and rainy days," he replied. Everyone laughed and gave Ed a big round of applause.

Martha had made special blankets and quilts for the little bed. She asked Edna to give her a hand with making the baby bed up. After the bed was ready, she took Homer and laid him in it. He was now lying in a bed of his own.

"Where is Jules?" asked Ollie.

"Would you believe your brother has bought him a horse and buggy? He will be on later. He wanted to go by to pick up Sally, and bring her for a spell. Looks like they are getting mighty stuck on one another," said Ed.

"Ollie, honey, Tom and I will be going home after supper. You have your folks and friends with you now and we will make room for them," said Mattie.

"Thank you for everything. Just as soon as I can travel we will be by to see you," replied Ollie.

The winter came in with a blast. Bill had done a good job preparing for it. Even though things were hectic at times with the accident and the baby coming, he never lost focus on what was necessary to keep things going well for his family. They really did enjoy the wintertime, especially with little Homer. He made each day special and exciting, as they learned how to take care of a baby. They had a bountiful harvest and were able to pay off all their debts. The bank had settled with them, and now the farm would be theirs, as they paid off the mortgage in the years to come. Ollie and Bill were closer to each other than ever before. The snow was whiter than Ollie could ever remember. The fire in the fireplace was not only good for cooking with the special pots and pans, but also it was nice to sit around the fire and pop popcorn and roast peanuts. The winter months was a great time to be together, and share their love with little Homer.

Early spring was poking its head out everywhere. Buds were on the trees, and jonquils had started shooting up from the ground. Spring was everywhere you looked and the weather was getting nice and warm. Ollie was glad she was able to walk with very little pain. Little Homer, now five months old, was really a joy for her. He was the main reason she was doing as well as she was. He kept her so busy; she didn't have time to think of her condition as much.

Bill came in from the barn and asked Ollie if she wanted to ride with him to Dawsonville tomorrow. It was time for them to let the rest of the town's people see their son, and for her to face the other folks, which hadn't seen her since the accident.

"I would like to, but don't you think it might be a little early to have the baby out and us going that far?"

"Not at all," he replied, "it will give us a chance to show him off to the town folks. We can stop by your folks on our way back too."

That got Ollie excited; knowing she would see her folks. It had been several months since she last saw them. She had gotten word, that Jules had asked Sally to marry him, and she had accepted his proposal.

———

"Ollie, Ollie," Bill was hollering out. "Where are you?"

She was startled as she heard the voice of Bill coming from the direction of the house. She didn't realize time had passed so quickly. She was still leaning against the cow holding onto the milk bucket. Bill made his way down the path to the barn, limping, and favoring his right hip, caused by all the years of hard work. He was pleased to see his Ollie in the stall, safe, and milking the cow.

"I was worried about you. When you didn't answer me, my heart almost stopped. My mind went back to that awful day I found you in the barn, when the cow had hurt you."

She finished milking, picked up her stool, the milk bucket, and stepped outside the stall. After closing the stall door, Bill took the milk pail in one hand, and put his other arm around his Ollie, as they slowly walked the path headed for the house.

"You know Ollie, since that time, we've had ten beautiful children, five boys and five girls," said Bill, as he let his arm slide down, patting her bottom with a soft tap.

Ollie's mind went back to the day when she had said to Edna, "I wonder if Bill will still love me, with my chest caved in, and my back like it is?"

End

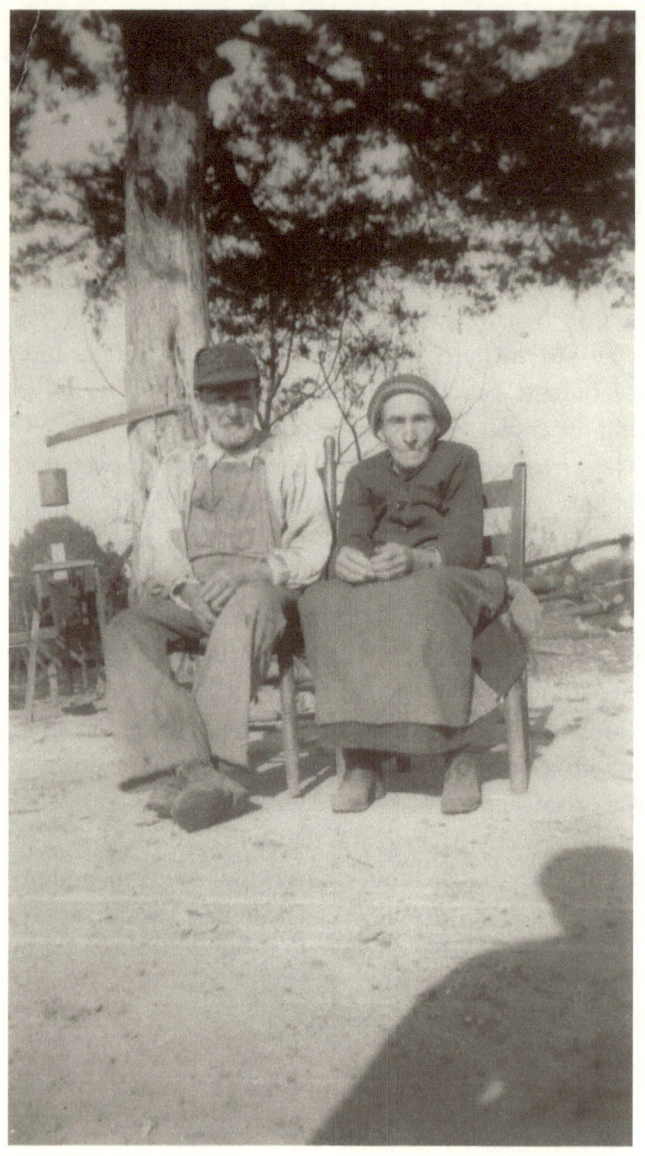

Ollie, a sixteen year old stepping out into adulthood sharing her love with her husband Bill and everything around her. Her life changed forever the morning she had to milk the cow. The cow filled with rage and hate, attack Ollie that fateful morning crushing her body and almost taking her life. That day changed Ollie's body and way of life forever.